For
Simone and Sarah

Lovers, Queens and Strangers

Strong Women in Celtic Myth

Anne Bernard Kearney

A. & A. Farmar

© Text Anne Bernard Kearney 1999
© Illustrations on pages 20, 40, 66, 80, 112
Anne Bernard Kearney 1999
© Cover illustration Carmel Benson 1999

First Published in 1999 by
A. & A. Farmar
Beech House
78 Ranelagh Village
Dublin 6
Ireland
Tel: + 353 1 496 3625 Fax: + 353 1 497 0107
Email: afarmar@iol.ie
All rights reserved. No text or illustration may be reproduced in any medium or storage system without permission from the publishers.

ISBN 1-899047-50-6

Lovers, Queens and Strangers is based on *Six femmes celtes* by Anne Bernard Kearney published by les Editions de l'Herne, Paris, 1996. The orthography of the Irish legends varies from text to text. In this retelling some names have been anglicised e.g. Medhbh is Maeve, Derbforgaill is Dervorgilla.

The illustrations by the author are scanned from etchings printed in the Graphic Studio, Dublin.

contents

Acknowledgements 6

Introduction 7

The Invincibility of Maeve 21

The Desire of Gráinne 41

The Daring of Deirdre 65

The Ruse of Emer 79

The Isolation of Dervorgilla 99

The Enchantment of Edain 105

Bibliography 138

acknowledgements

I wish to thank all those who helped me with this book: my mother, Kathleen Fitzpatrick Bernard who introduced me to the marvels of Irish literature when I was growing up in France; Richard Kearney for his unfailing support; my daughters Simone and Sarah for their encouraging presence; Joe O'Leary, Marina Warner, Luke Gibbons and Declan Kiberd who read the manuscript and made useful comments; Nuala Ní Dhomhnaill, Proinsias Mac Cana, Marie Heaney, Angela Bourke, the late Liam de Paor, Tomás Ó Cathasaigh, Caoimhín Mac Giolla Leith and Margaret MacCurtain who shared with me their rich knowledge of the original Gaelic sources or were greatly encouraging; those who helped me in different ways with the French version of the book: Stanislas Breton, Claude Mettra, Jean Greisch, Pierre Johannet and Alexandre Defay; Mary Condren for her generosity in introducing me to the story of Dervorgilla and opening many vistas on Celtic women and culture; finally my deep gratitude to Anna and Tony Farmar for their commitment to this work.

Anne Bernard Kearney
June 1999

Introduction

'Home lies ahead, in the unfolding of the story in the future, not behind waiting to be regained.'

Marina Warner *Managing Monsters: Six Myths of our Time*

Six women shine out in the Irish Celtic legends, for their strength, their character, their audacity—Maeve, Gráinne, Deirdre, Emer, Dervorgilla and Edain. They are described as the most beautiful women in Ireland, full of grace, wisdom and fine speech. Moreover, they know how to engage in combat, like Maeve and how to use their hands with dexterity and competence like Emer. They are music makers and know how to heal like Edain, they are full of vitality and ardour like Deirdre, they are exceptionally attractive like Dervorgilla and full of pride and audacity like Gráinne.

These women with guttural names—are they goddesses, heroines or ordinary women? What is their strength, their secret? What can they tell us today? How do they answer the perennial question: 'What do women want?'

In Arthurian legend, the answer to this ques-

Lovers, Queens and Strangers

tion is 'sovereignty': to be self-possessed, unbeholden to others, unsubmissive, free to determine one's destiny and follow one's desires.

How do these women express their sovereignty, their self-possession?

Maeve is headstrong, at times ferocious; she owes nothing to anybody. Confident in her power and wealth, she is generous and needs a husband with qualities equal to her own, who is not jealous or mean or fearful. When one of her bulls deserts her for her husband's stables (not willing to be subject to a woman!), Maeve will not rest until she acquires another one of equal size. Warrior queen, uncontested in her own territory, she goes to war for this bull. Her urine scours the landscape and her menstrual blood cuts three deep ravines big enough to

Introduction

contain three households. Her sensuality is unparalleled: she boasts of always having 'one man in the shadow of another'. Maeve's sovereignty is shown in her indomitable willpower.

Gráinne expresses her sovereign character in her readiness to change. Unlike Deirdre who remains faithful to her lover after his death, Gráinne adapts to each new circumstance. Although she has agreed to marry Finn, the chief of the Fianna, she changes her mind on her wedding day, finding him too old for her liking. She chooses Oisín instead; then Diarmuid, on whom she casts her *geis* or spell. Finally, she returns to Finn, Diarmuid's rival, reaffirming her fidelity to life, to survival.

Deirdre rejects the king who tries to force himself on her as a husband. Instead, she chooses to love a young man with hair as black as a crow, with cheeks as red as blood, with skin as pale as snow. Vivacious, impulsive and determined, Deirdre uses the mysterious power of the *geis* to compel the young Naisi to run away with her. She ignores the prediction made at her birth and flees into exile with her lover. Defiance is the hallmark of her sovereignty.

Emer is intelligent and artistic, gifted with her hands. Knowing that her father will do all in his power to oppose her marriage she replies in riddles to the hero who courts her. She weaves words as finely as she weaves threads. Faced with a rival, Fand, she negotiates with speech rather than weapons. Her power is based in wit and discernment.

Dervorgilla comes from another country in search of her lover. But when the man she chooses cannot marry her, she asks him to be her friend. She wins a competition of bodily fluids with one hundred and fifty-three queens of Ireland when they urinate on a pillar of snow but only her urine reaches the ground. Her rivals avenge themselves in a hideous way. By her courage in revealing herself as different, as singular, Dervorgilla demonstrates her sovereignty.

Finally, *Edain* possesses a quiet, persistent strength with her mysterious shape-shifting power. She turns herself into an insect that changes size. Even in this form, she knows how to heal and how to give happiness. Later she will multiply into fifty Edains like herself, to put the king who courts her to the test. It is only by uniting himself with her that the king acquires sovereignty. Edain confers this power, disclosing her sovereignty by this capacity for metamorphosis.

These mythological women, now fairy, now human, move freely from one world to another, from the sacred to the profane, from the

Introduction

Otherworld to the earthly plane. They represent three major functions—magic, vitality, and fertility—which correspond in turn to the three roles identified by George Dumézil: priestess-poet, sorceress-warrior and lover-nurturer. As Proinsias Mac Cana explains in *Celtic Mythology*:

'The first function concerns the administration of the universe and has two aspects, the one magico-religious, the other rational and judicial ... The second consists in the exercise of physical force, "primarily but not solely of a warlike nature".... The third comprises all the manifestations of the notion of fertility: prosperity, health, fecundity in plant and animal life, peace, voluptuousness and numerical weight.'

Magic

The magical power of these Celtic women is displayed through the *geis* and through the power of the word.

Geis or *geas* is 'a solemn injunction especially of a magical kind, the infringement of which led to misfortune or even death', according to Dinneen's Irish–English dictionary. It is like 'an unconditional prohibition, a sort of categorical imperative of magical character', writes Marie-Louise Sjoestedt in *Gods and Heroes*. In these legends a *geis* is a binding power, a taboo, often imposed by a woman, which isolates or protects the king or the hero and can ultimately be the cause of his death if he does not comply with it. The *geis* is a form of impersonal magical interdict that can take many forms. It is a supernatural force, belonging to the world of fairies. The *geis* can be interpreted as a ritual means of dispensing with the king or the hero, and so is perhaps an alternative way of exercising sovereignty—oblique and indirect, but effective.

While women are not subject to *geis*, they have the power to impose one on the hero of their choice. When Gráinne asks Diarmuid to be her companion and he refuses, she imposes a *geis* on him. He has to obey, otherwise he would forfeit his honour. In absconding with Gráinne he commits a double offence: he abandons the night-watch of the fortress and betrays his chief, Finn, to whom Gráinne is betrothed. Gráinne's *geis* overrides Diarmuid's deep warrior bond with his companions and chief, and even his immediate duty.

Another example of the *geis* is Deirdre's challenge to Naisi to elope with her: she takes him by the two ears, and says: 'Shame on you if you don't take me with you!' Having refused to marry the old and possessive king, the young and fiery Deirdre flees with Naisi, who only

introduction

consents in order to avoid the shame and derision which he would face if he did not accept the challenge. This challenge is linked to the theme of 'elopement' from the paternal house, a theme which has great importance in Celtic legends. The *geis* recurs, for instance, when Emer threatens Lugaid, displaying the same kind of defiance in protecting herself from a forced marriage.

In these legends the *geis* appears to be a feminine power used to attract men, to bind them and keep them in check. The women know that it is stronger than any other force: since it involves honour it touches the most vulnerable point of the heroic conscience and overrules all else. Thus women have access to an authority higher even than the demands of honour, though apparently without a transcendent source.

An analogous power is that of the *word*. For example, Gráinne uses the magic force of words to put Finn in his place. Levorcham, Deirdre's wise woman companion, is gifted with the genius of speech and satire. She is a poet and tells Deirdre where she can find the man of her dreams. Through language these Celtic women can transform things, attack men's honour and even threaten life if what they demand is not granted.

The women are not passive muses turned towards the past or some lost golden age: they look to the future with energy and resolution.

Metamorphosis

Metamorphosis (shape-shifting) is another recurrent theme. Dervorgilla and her handmaid transform themselves into swans. Edain, turned into a pool of water by a jealous woman, mutates into a worm, then into a beautiful insect. In this form, she wins the fidelity of two men, Midir and Aengus. Later she is reborn a new woman, changes into a swan and flies out of an opening in the roof, escaping the king. Finally, she completes her series of metamorphoses by multiplying into fifty women like herself, identical in features and clothing.

These metamorphoses suggest an openness to multiple possibilities of being, a certain freedom, the freedom to adapt, to overcome what is given in order to affirm what is different and new. There is also perhaps a link between metamorphosis and transgression. Edain becomes an insect; the word used for insect in Gaelic, *cuil*, is very close to the word for incest, *col*. The phenomenon of metamorphosis raises the age-old question of the unique and the double. The fact that one of the fifty Edain-like

introduction

women is her own daughter, is like a challenge, a wager of multiple identities. Which is the true and original, which the fake or copy? Which is the mother, which the daughter?

The theme of metamorphosis is also often linked to repetition. Edain is born twice, with one thousand and twelve years between births; she has two loves, as if in the repetition there is a possibility of completing something only half begun in the past, retrieving or redeeming it in the present.

Metamorphosis also suggests abundance, ever-renewing resources and the blurring of boundaries as where the sea meets the sky in the haze of the horizon.

Fertility

These Celtic women are remarkable for the liberty of their sexual lives. Maeve beds so many men that she can hardly count them. She offers herself to the man who will give her the brown bull of Ulster. Gráinne's sensuality is audacious; she taunts Diarmuid, saying that he, the valiant warrior, is less daring than the water in the river which laps her thighs.

But the sexual autonomy of these women is apparent in their restraint as well as in their licence. Maeve takes pleasure in reciting the

Lovers, Queens and Strangers

names of those she has rejected. Gráinne refuses all the champions and kings' sons who court her. Emer is faithful to her promise of chastity: when Lugaid seeks to marry her, she declares that Cúchulainn is her only love. Deirdre, crushed by sorrow after Naisi's death, kills herself when the king offers her to her enemy. Gráinne, too, remains faithful, loving Diarmuid until he dies. Edain, choosing between Midir and Eochaid, agrees to follow the king of the Otherworld, Midir, if his rival, Eochaid, the king of Ireland, gives his consent. She plays fair. Later, she appears to Eochaid, who is fighting to win her back, under the guise of fifty indistinguishable Edains. Only if the king can recognise her will he win her. In each case, Edain is in command of her sexual relationships with men.

Motifs of fecundity and of erotic prowess are prominent in these stories. They are sometimes represented by the flow of bodily fluids. Dervorgilla's water goes through the pillar of snow, melting it and reaching the ground. Her ardour and her fertility make her superior to the queens who plot her destruction. Maeve passes water on the floor of her tent as she is speaking to Ailill, a sign of freedom and sensuous vitality. The places where Maeve uri-

Introduction

nated still bear her name, in accord with the Celtic pattern whereby goddesses are linked to landscape, to the spirit of the place, while gods are more linked to historical myths. Similarly, Maeve's periods cut deep ravines in the ground and she even leaves the shelter of shields on the battlefield, without shame, to let her menstrual blood flow.

Finally, four of the myths show an obvious link between sexuality and fertility, a link that also bears on the practice of sovereignty. Maeve, Gráinne, Edain and Dervorgilla are all mothers. This fertility is important not only in demonstrating fecundity, but in the extension of the women's power through their offspring. Maeve sends her children to the battlefield, while Gráinne asks hers to travel the world to acquire the knowledge of arms necessary to avenge her. These women do not feel their mothering is simply in the service of manhood, they do not question themselves about their fertility or feel they have to have children in order to be sovereign. Confident in their bodies, in their desirability, in themselves, they do not act as subordinates to men or gods.

The women's power lies partly in their capacity to provoke an irresistible desire in men, partly in the sheer abundance of their own, sometimes ferocious, sexual appetite and partly in the power of their bodily fluids which hold the masculine at bay. But their strength does not exclude wisdom. They are worldly-wise, practical, prudent; and they know how to live. In these stories there are no allusions to Christianity or a precise religious system and no trace of a moral system, in the strict sense of the word.

We are far from monotheism here, or from those divinities who order the fate of mortals from above as in Greco-Roman mythology. It could be said that with these women, sovereignty expresses itself in the dynamic formula: 'I can therefore I am.' Each in her own way teaches us something unique about the attainment of sovereignty. As Marina Warner remarks in *Six Myths of our Time:*

'This motley, mongrel, volatile character of folklore is of crucial importance, because even while stories are patently connected to particular places and peoples, as in the case of Hindu epics or the Irish legends, they aren't immutable. They're not even recuperable in some imagined integrity, because the act of recuperation itself and the context of the retelling affect the interpretation.'

What follows is not a description or an ex-

Introduction

planation of the myths but rather a retelling, based on edited passages of the legends, with reflections on their meaning for women in our time. These versions invite readers to reinterpret for themselves. I have tried to listen anew to the stories, and to hear what they have to say to us about our lives today; to take from them what is original and distinct, while avoiding anachronism yet remaining open to the unique images they evoke.

The six women I have chosen stand out from the many other women in these texts by virtue of their singular self-possession. I have approached them not as objects of antique curiosity—mystic creatures of some Celtic twilight—but as living subjects in their own right.

Lovers, Queens and Strangers

Some time afterwards, at the height of the battle to win the bul[l] Maeve allowed her menstrual blood to flow on the battlefield. He[r] gush of blood was so powerful that it dug three channels wide enoug[h] to contain three households. And this place is known to this day a[s] 'Maeve's stain'.

the invincibility of maeve

One morning, Queen Maeve and King Ailill were enjoying a moment of pillow talk on Maeve's royal bed in the castle of Cruachain.

'Don't you agree with the saying,' said Ailill, 'that lucky is the wife of a rich man?'

'I do, but what brings this to your mind?'

'I was thinking that you are much better-off since you became my wife.'

'I was just as wealthy before our wedding day!'

'Yes indeed you were rich, but who knew it? You were a woman of wealth and your neighbours could steal from you as much they pleased.'

'On the contrary: my father, Eochu Feidlech mac Find meic Findomain meic Findeoin (going back ten generations) was the great king of Ireland. He fathered six daughters amongst whom I was the noblest, the most attractive, the most gifted. The best on the battlefield, in strife and in combat. My mercenaries, all sons of exiles and of free men of the country, were legion. That is why my father gave me one of the provinces of Ireland, Cruachain. And I was named Maeve of Cruachain. How many kings wanted to wed me! Find, king of Leinster, Cairbre, king of Tara, Conor, king of Ulster. But I did not want any of them, for I imposed one condition which no woman before me had ever thought of: I wanted a man without miserliness, without jealousy, and without fear.

'If the man of my choice had been miserly, how ill-matched we would have been, for I am generous! What would people have said? That my generosity surpassed his! He would have lost face. But where there is equal generosity, no grounds of reproach are found.

'Nor, if my husband had been timorous, would we have been well matched. For I fight battles, jousts and combats all on my own and always win. How bad it would be for my husband to have a woman braver than he! But who would find fault in a couple of equal courage?

'As for jealousy, I've had one man in the shadow of another!'

Maeve ended by saying: 'So it is I who found you, Ailill, son of Ross Ruad of Leinster. You are neither miserly, nor jealous, nor fearful. I gave you a contract, and a wedding gift of twelve cloaks for men, a cart worth three times seven *cumals,* the width of your face in gold, and the weight of your left arm in white bronze. If anyone shames you, makes trouble for you, or embarrasses you, you can only claim in compensation what I would declare, for you are a husband dependent on my dowry.'

Ailill cried out that it wasn't so, that he had two brothers, Find and Cairbre, to whom he had left the crown, not because they were richer or more gifted than he, but simply because they were older. 'I never heard of a province governed by a woman,' he said, 'I came here to assume the role of king by virtue of my mother's rights, for my mother was Mata Muirisc, daughter of Magadu Connacht. And who could be, for me, a better queen than you, the daughter of the High King of Ireland?'

'No matter what you say,' Maeve answered

back, 'my wealth surpasses yours!'

'Not so. There is no wealth superior to mine, I know it well.'

And so they listed their respective belongings, comparing riches with riches, item by item, from the most insignificant to the most precious. They left nothing out: pottery, cauldrons, basins, jewellery, clothes, even mentioning the colours. Then each head of each herd was counted. After the count they reckoned that their possessions were equal in size and number. But amongst Ailill's herd was a very special bull which had been the calf of one of Maeve's cows. His name was Finnbennach, which means 'white horn'. But this bull had deemed it beneath his dignity to belong to a woman. He had left Maeve's herd and joined Ailill's. But for Maeve, not to possess a similar bull in her stable was worse than possessing nothing.

So Maeve called her chamberlain, Fergus, and asked him to find her a bull of equal proportions.

'I can find you an even better bull. His name is Donn Cuailnge, the Brown Bull of Cuailnge.

He belongs to Daire in Ulster,' said Fergus.

'Ask Daire to lend me his bull for a year. At the end of the year he will receive the price of one year's use, that is fifty heifers. And of course the bull himself will be returned. Tell him also, Fergus, that if people in the area have objections to this special loan, he may come here with his bull. I will give him a territory of the same size as his own territory, a chariot worth three times seven *cumals*. And the warmth of my thighs.'

With this mission, Fergus's men went to Ulster. Fergus explained the reason for his coming to Daire, who did not hide his joy and promised to lend the bull whatever the Ulster people thought about it. But while they were celebrating the success of their mission, regaling themselves with abundance of food and drink, Fergus's men started gossiping. They said that Daire's generosity was indeed remarkable, but that a refusal to let the bull go would not have stopped Maeve: what a carnage there might have been! Their words were overheard and repeated to Daire who took offence and changed his mind: 'I swear by the holy gods that only by force will they get what they can no longer gain by straight asking!'

When Fergus's men, ignorant of this turn of events, inquired next morning about the whereabouts of the bull, they were astonished by Daire's answer: 'If it was customary of me to ill-treat messengers or travellers, you would leave here feet first!' Seeing their puzzled expression, he continued: 'You said that if I hadn't agreed to give the bull to you, I would be forced to let him go under the pressure of Maeve's army led by Fergus.'

'You mustn't hold against Maeve what is said under the influence of good food and drink', said Fergus.

'I have decided. I am not giving you the bull.'

On their return to Connacht, Fergus told Maeve what had happened. 'Don't bother to smooth it over, Fergus,' she said, 'it was obvious this bull was not going to be given up except by force. And that is what will happen.'

Maeve asked her seven sons, all named

Maine, to return with their seven divisions of three thousand men. Fergus and another king came as well with three thousand men. They set up camp in front of Cruachain and held festivities for two weeks in preparation for the march. Then Maeve had her horses harnessed so that she could go and consult her druid about the future of her expedition.

Maeve said to the druid: 'Many of those embarking on this journey today are leaving behind friends, land, father and mother, and if they do not come back healthy and safe, their resentment will fall upon me. Moreover, there isn't one who is leaving today who isn't dearer to us than ourselves. Tell us if we shall be amongst those who will return.' The druid spoke: 'Whatever happens to the others, you will come home.'

On the way back to Cruachain, Maeve had an extraordinary vision: a woman dressed in a cloak with green dots, attached by a heavy brooch above her breast, appeared before her. She was weaving a fringe with a white bronze spindle in her right hand. Her eyes were smiling, her lips were red like rubies, her teeth were pearls in her mouth. Her speech was soft as the sound of the harp. Her long blond hair was divided into three plaits, two twined around her head, the third hanging freely down her back to her knees.

Maeve, fascinated, asked what she was doing there. The woman replied that she was watching over Maeve's interest and prosperity, that she was helping her to rally the other great provinces of Ireland to go to Ulster in quest of the Brown Bull of Cuailgne.

'Why are you doing this for me?' asked Maeve.

'I have a reason, I am the servant of your people.'

'Who are you?' Maeve asked.

'I am the prophetess Feidelm of the Otherworld of Cruachain.'

Maeve asked her then how she saw her army.

'I see it red, I see it purple.'

Maeve said the time for battle was good because it was the period during which her enemies, the warriors of Ulster, lay prostrate suffering the pangs of Macha. These pangs were the result of a curse laid upon the sons of Ulster by a fairy woman called Macha who died after a great contest, giving birth to twins. Before she died she vowed that the men of Ulster would suffer similar labour pains when they were most in need of strength. There was no more to fear from that quarter! Nevertheless, Maeve asked again about her own army.

'I see it red, I see it purple,' repeated Feidelm.

Maeve, annoyed, spoke again of the pangs of Macha which were affecting all the warriors of the province. But Feidelm did not alter her answer, not the third time, nor the fourth, nor the sixth time the question was asked. Maeve, losing patience, said that the men of Ireland always fell into discord, that they did not know how to agree on who would head a convoy, on who would cross a ford first, on who would give the first blow to an animal.

'I see it red, I see it purple,' the prophetess repeated.

Then Feidelm revealed her vision in a song: she described the beauty of a young hero whose eyes were precious stone, and whose virtue and charm attracted the love of women. Could it

Lovers, Queens and Strangers

be Cúchulainn? But she knew one thing: the army of Maeve would suffer from Cúchulainn's blows. With his sword, Gae Bulga, this young man with a red cloak would have a foot in each battlefield.

'He will defeat your entire army, he will be the cause of the killings, you will leave him all your men . . . The blood will spill, it will be remembered for a long time. Bodies of men torn to pieces, women weeping . . .'

The first night of the march towards Ulster, Maeve, distrustful, passed through the camps in her chariot. She wanted to hear the prophecies, and to know who was participating in the expedition out of his own free will and who recoiled from it. She came back impressed, but alarmed at the speed and efficiency of one of the allied armies: the Galeons. The other armies were hardly beginning to pitch their tents when the Galeons were already preparing their meal, and they had finished it before any of the armies had time to start theirs. Ailill saw nothing amiss with such devoted allies, but

Maeve refused to let them join her armies.

'Let them stay at home then!' said Ailill. Maeve refused.

'What can they do, if they can neither join us nor stay at home?'

'I want all of them dead!' roared Maeve unflinchingly. For she was afraid that the Galeons might attract all the glory or that they might unite against her.

Fergus was the guarantor of the Galeons and took it upon himself to defend them, even if he had to pay with his own blood. Maeve agreed to his suggestion that these soldiers be spread out amongst other armies so that they would never be more than five together.

'Anything,' was Maeve's response, 'provided those Galeons don't retain the power they have now!' So Fergus divided them amongst the warriors of the four provinces of Ireland.

Maeve then succeeded in dividing each of the remaining armies under the pretext that they could not all advance on the same road. She advised Ailill to take some of them on the Midluachair road, while she and Fergus would take another route.

Lovers, Queens and Strangers

Ailill suspected that great intimacy existed between Maeve and Fergus and asked his chariot driver, Cuillius, to spy on them.

Soon enough, Cuillius found Maeve and Fergus on top of one another at Cluithre, where they had lingered while the army marched on. They were so busy that he could come near them without being seen or heard. Fergus's sword was lying close to the couple. Cuillius stole it out of the sheath.

Cuillus found Ailill and confirmed his suspicions. 'It doesn't matter,' said King Ailill. They looked at one another with an understanding smile. And he added: 'I understand that she does it to preserve Fergus's fidelity to us. Keep the sword. Put it under your seat, hidden in some clothes.'

Fergus discovered his sword was missing. 'It is terrible,' he said to Maeve.

'What are you saying?' said Maeve.

'The wrong I've done to Ailill,' said Fergus. He searched in vain for his sword in the forest. He then cut a wooden sword for himself and met Ailill, who bade him welcome. They played chess, talking about infidelity.

But it was Maeve who had the last word: 'Let it be, let us forget it.'

A short time later, Maine, one of Maeve and Ailill's sons, wanted to venture out in combat. Fergus tried to keep him back and, fearful for his life, offered to go himself. But Maeve said she wanted Fergus to stay to watch over the herd with his army.

Maine and thirty horsemen met their death at the ford of the river Cronn, where Cúchulainn had been waiting. Many other sons also found their deaths. Later, Maeve, impulsive and confident of victory, did not hesitate to offer two of her remaining sons to help Ferdia in his combat against Cúchulainn.

Maeve, in the hopes of winning Ferdia over, had promised him her daughter, Finnabair, in marriage and much wealth besides. Even, if he wished, the friendliness of her own thighs! Faced with his refusal, she ended up by provoking him to engage in a fight with his half-brother Cúchulainn, saying that he, Cúchulainn, despised him as a warrior. When Ferdia came to bid Maeve farewell, he found her urinating freely on the floor of her tent. Some time afterwards, at the height of the battle to win the bull, Maeve allowed her menstrual blood to flow on the battlefield. Her gush of blood was so powerful that it dug three channels wide enough to contain three households. And this place is known to this day as 'Maeve's stain'.

Fergus said at last: 'It was foolish of us to follow the rump of a woman. Everybody knows that a herd led by a mare deserves to be crushed.'

But Cúchulainn, who fell upon her as she was squatting, had not dared to kill her. Maeve made peace with Cúchulainn and returned to her home.

And Finnbennach, the bull with the white horn who had left Maeve's stable at the beginning because he refused to belong to a woman, met his end that day under the blows of the brown bull, whose heart then burst.

On Maeve

Maeve is one of the most illustrious Celtic queens. Her name means 'one who intoxicates'. She is a formidable warrior queen, a woman larger than life, who always has one man 'in the shadow of the other'. On the battlefield, she is a courageous woman whom nothing stops. Maeve can be devious, ruthless, manipulative; she does not hesitate to stir up dissension and conflict.

Her name probably comes from the ritual of sovereignty wherein the newly installed king had to drink an inebriating draught from a goblet. She is also identified as a goddess of fecundity. Maeve has eight children whom she does not hesitate to use to defend her interests, without concern for their lives.

Maeve is sexually free: the men with whom she sleeps are innumerable. She marries several times (seven according to some accounts), and discards husbands who do not interest her any more. She has no doubts about her power of seduction, offering her thighs to whoever will give her the bull she seeks. This is read in different ways, 'It is precisely in her breaches of propriety that we find the clearest evidence of Maeve's divinity; her licentiousness is merely the literary expression of one of the characteristic functions of the Celtic goddess,' says Proinsias Mac Cana in Celtic Mythology *(p. 85). She does not conceal her lovemaking with her war companion, Fergus, whom her husband's charioteer, Cuillius, finds perched 'on her royal belly', nor does she hesitate to relieve herself of her 'gush of blood' which is so abundant it creates ravines deep enough to contain three households. For some commentators, such as Mary Condren and Marion Deane, this story illustrates the incompatibility of war and menstruation. I prefer to see here an act of singular freedom, for are not her bodily fluids incredibly powerful? The two acts of urinating and letting blood flow freely are acts of detachment or scorn, rather than an admission of weakness. They are sovereign rather than shameful acts.*

Maeve does not want to owe anything to anyone. Re-installing equality between her hus-

band and herself is a matter of principle and equity: she wants the material proof that she owes Ailill nothing, that her marriage to him did not in any way increase her wealth, did not make her a kept woman. Maeve and Ailill make inventories of their respective goods. They are equally wealthy except for one bull who formerly belonged to Maeve. (And as has been said by anthropologists about other European and Indian myths, the bull symbolises the warrior function.) But this bull, named Finnbennach, the One with the White Horn, had left her for the king's stables, deeming it beneath his dignity to be under a woman's authority. Thus Maeve needs to acquire a bull of the same strength and size to re-establish equality with Ailill. But as he dies in the end might he not have done better to stay in Maeve's stable?

Maeve is an autonomous queen, sovereign in her own land, Connacht, in her own fort, Cruachain (today in County Roscommon). It is Ailill who came to her, not the other way round. She works hard at keeping a close hand on her domain whatever the price and despite all opposition.

Maeve personifies sovereignty, making 'kings out of the men who, without her, would not obtain this rank', writes George Dumézil in Mythe et Epopée *(p. 331, translation by the author). He recognises this in the qualities she demands of her partner: that he be 'without jealousy, fear or meanness': this represents a psychological expression of the structures of the famous 'three functions' (sovereignty, strength, fertility). Those three qualities are absolutely necessary for the 'balance of a society and the success of a reign'. To be jealous would mean to 'morbidly fear rivals, controls, resistance' a vice belonging to 'tyranny under all its aspects, judicial as well as political'. Jealousy is an unacceptable quality in a judge, as cowardice is in a warrior and meanness in a farmer. In Proinsias Mac Cana's words: 'The qualities of a rightful king (which in Irish are comprised under the term* fir flaithemhan, *literally "truth of the ruler") are reflected in the condition of his kingdom. They ensure peace and equity, security of the kingdom's borders, and material prosperity: the trees bend low with the weight of their fruit, the rivers and the sea teem with abundance of fish, and the earth brings forth rich harvests.'* (Celtic Mythology *p. 119*)

Maeve reserves the right to refuse any partner, even a king, who does not possess those three qualities. Ailill, her fourth husband, meets these requirements, and she bears him seven sons and a daughter, Finnabair. According to Dumézil, Maeve personifies one of the various forms of flaith *or power. He points, moreover, to the assonance of the words 'power' (*flaith*) and 'beer' (*(f)laith*). To become king depends on a certain intoxicating drink, 'a red beer' or 'red sovereignty'. Dumézil also remarks that with Maeve, Ireland (as opposed to Celtic Britain) entrusted the royal function or the health of the king,* rí *and* ardrí, *to a woman who was far from the ideal virgin.*

Maeve seems to incarnate sovereignty by her lack of jealousy, fear and meanness. In other words, by her independence of mind, her warrior courage and her fertile sensuality.

lovers, queens and strangers

One day, as they were crossing a stream, a splash of water reached the top of her thighs. Gráinne said she was astonished that such a valiant and audacious warrior as Diarmuid could be so shy and controlled in matters of love.

The Desire of Gráinne

1 The Pursuit

On the day that she was to marry Finn mac Cumhaill, the chief of the Fianna, in Almu, his fortress in Leinster, Gráinne seduced Diarmuid. It happened during the banquet, when all the chiefs of Ireland were seated at the table of her father, Cormac, the High King of Ireland. Gráinne was amazed that Finn, who was older than her father, had proposed himself as a husband. Why had he not suggested his son instead?

Gráinne filled a cup with a magical brew and offered it to Finn and most of the rest of the company. They all fell into a deep sleep. She addressed the two men whom she hadn't served: Diarmuid, the warrior with the soft talk, the red cheeks and the black hair, and his friend Oisín, Finn's son. Gráinne stood up gracefully and spoke to Oisín first:

Lovers, Queens and Strangers

'I cannot understand why Finn wants a woman like me. Rather than having a man older than my father, I would like one who would be my equal.'

'Do not speak like that, Gráinne,' said Oisín. 'If Finn heard you, he would not want you any more, and as for me, I would not dare take you.'

'Do you agree that I should court you, Oisín?' Gráinne asked.

'No. No matter who she is, I cannot touch a woman promised to my father!'

Gráinne turned towards Diarmuid, the warrior with black hair and the love spot on his forehead: 'And you, Diarmuid, will you let me court you, since Oisín refuses?'

'No,' replied Diarmuid, 'even if you weren't Finn's betrothed, I could not take Oisín's.'

'Then I will put a *geis* on you,' said Gráinne. 'I will put you under a curse if you don't take me with you this very night! Take me far away from here before Finn and the king wake up!'

'By what a bad spell you bind me!' exclaimed Diarmuid. 'Why do that to me, this evening, in front of all the chiefs and in the house of the king? There is no man who deserves less to

gráinne

be loved than me!'

'But Diarmuid, it is not without reason that I put this spell on you!' She reminded him of a sporting encounter on the plain in front of the fort. From her window she had observed him marking three goals against the warriors of Tara.

'From that day on, I gave my love to no other, and I never will.'

'I am surprised nevertheless that it is me and not Finn that you love. Do you know that there isn't a man in the whole of Ireland who makes love to women better than he, and moreover, it is he who has the keys of the fort! It is impossible for us to leave.'

'We will leave through the hidden door in my room,' answered Gráinne.

'I am not permitted to use such a door,' protested Diarmuid.

'Like any warrior, you can leap over the rampart of a fortress with your wooden lance. I will go through the small door. You will follow me.'

Gráinne left. Diarmuid asked Oisín for his advice: 'What can I do now that this *geis* has been imposed on me?'

Lovers, Queens and Strangers

'It is not your fault, Diarmuid! I advise you to follow Gráinne and to protect yourself from Finn's anger.' It was well known that only a fool would ignore a *geis*. Diarmuid had to leave with Gráinne, although he would probably meet his death.

Diarmuid stood up and took his arms. If blueberries had fallen from his eyes when he bade farewell they would not have been bigger than his tears. When he reached the rampart, he leapt over it like a bird with the help of his lance, a leap so powerful, so high that he landed on his two feet on the green grass of the plain where Gráinne came to meet him.

'This is a bad road that you make us take, Gráinne. Why choose me when it was Finn who was meant to be your lover? I do not know where we can hide in Ireland! Go back, there is time yet, Finn will know nothing.'

'No, I will never go back. Only death can take me from you.'

'Come then,' said Diarmuid.

They had not travelled a mile when Gráinne started to complain about being tired.

'It's a good thing this is happening now, it's

gráinne

not too late to return to the fort. For one thing is certain, Gráinne: I give you my word as a warrior, never in all eternity will I carry you on my back!'

Having reached Doire Dá Both, Diarmuid created a clearing in the middle of the forest. He built a hut with seven little doors, and made a bed with water lilies and birch leaves.

When Finn woke up in his fortress and discovered Diarmuid and Gráinne had fled, his rage and his jealousy were beyond measure. He summoned his warrior-huntsmen and they all set out. Thus began the pursuit of Diarmuid and Gráinne.

As Diarmuid's companions wanted to protect him, they sent him several warnings. Gráinne took notice of these but Diarmuid refused to flee. Finn and the Fianna came upon them both in the forest. They were about to capture them, when Diarmuid publicly kissed Gráinne three times. Finn's jealousy and anger redoubled; he swore that Diarmuid would pay for those kisses with his head.

Aengus, Diarmuid's foster-father, saw what a perilous situation his foster-son had landed himself in and hastened to his rescue. Being visible only to Gráinne and Diarmuid, he asked them what had happened. Diarmuid replied: 'We fled from the king and Finn. But I wasn't the one who wanted this!' Aengus offered to take them far away under cover of his magic cloak.

Diarmuid, however, wanted to escape through his own resources. He let Gráinne go and promised to join them as soon as he could. Diarmuid made another of his prodigious bounds over the armies and rejoined Gráinne who was overjoyed to see him.

The next day, before taking his leave, Aengus told them how they could avoid their pursuers:

'On your flight, do not climb into a tree which has only one trunk. Do not seek refuge in a cave that has only one exit. Do not eat where you have prepared your food. Do not sleep where you have eaten. Do not rise where you lie down to sleep.'

Diarmuid and Gráinne pursued their path, remembering Aengus's advice.

Diarmuid had not yet made love to Gráinne.

gráinne

One day, as they were crossing a stream, a splash of water reached the top of her thighs. Gráinne said she was astonished that such a valiant and audacious warrior as Diarmuid could be so shy and controlled in matters of love. 'If it were a question of love, this spurt of water would be bolder than you are!' Then Diarmuid allowed his love to overcome his fear.

That evening, in their hut in the middle of the forest, they ate a deer Diarmuid had hunted and drank their fill. Early the next morning, Diarmuid paid a visit to the monster of the Tuatha Dé Danann, Searbán Lochlannach, one of the sons of the wicked Cham, son of Noah. The monster agreed to a pact that gave Diarmuid the right to hunt on his land as long as he did not touch the berries on his tree.

Some time later, Gráinne learned that the fruit of that tree had magical powers. 'What are these fruit?' she asked Diarmuid. 'They are magical berries from a tree that grew when the Tuatha Dé Danann dropped a berry brought from Tir Tairngire,' he replied. 'Whoever eats three of them will be protected from illness. They have the effect of wine and restore youth.

Even a hundred-year-old would return to the prime of youth after eating them. The monster who protects that tree has black skin and a large nose with crooked tusks. He has one red eye in the middle of his forehead. There is a thick collar around his giant's body. No weapon can wound him, no fire can burn him, no water can drown him. He cannot die unless struck by three strokes of his own iron club. He sleeps at the top of the tree, and he spends his day guarding it. He has transformed the country all around into a wilderness. I made a pact with this terrible one which allows me to hunt, provided I never touch one of the berries of that tree.'

On hearing this, Gráinne announced to Diarmuid that she would not share his bed unless she had tasted this fruit, though it was not wise for a woman with child as she was.

'I feel so heavy with this child I carry. I will die if I don't taste one of those berries!'

'Do not force me to break my peace with Searbán Lochlannach,' pleaded Diarmuid, 'it will not be easy for me to obtain them.' But Gráinne persuaded him.

gráinne

Diarmuid woke the giant up and asked him for a fistful of his berries for Gráinne. Searbán answered that even if the child in her womb, or Gráinne herself, were to die and their lineage were to stop there, he would never grant her a single berry. A fight could not be avoided. Diarmuid disarmed the giant and struck him three times with his club, dashing his brains out. When the hard battle was over Diarmuid said to Gráinne: 'Here are the berries you craved, gather as many as you please.' But she would eat only those he plucked with his own hands.

Diarmuid and Gráinne climbed into the rowan tree. They lay in the giant's bed. The berries of the lower branches seemed bitter after tasting the ones they had picked at the top.

Finn and the seven battalions of the Fianna learned that Diarmuid had taken the berries from the magic tree. They went to the giant's place. Finn, sensing Diarmuid's presence, camped at the foot of the tree. Finn and his son Oisín started to play chess in the great heat of noon. Despite Gráinne's plea, Diarmuid, who was observing the game from the top of the tree, helped his friend Oisín with berries adroitly aimed at the board. Finn discovered the couple suspended in the branches. And Diarmuid vexed Finn once more by giving Gráinne three kisses in full view of the whole army. Finn, more incensed by this public demonstration than by the elopement from Tara, swore again that Diarmuid would pay with his head.

He decided, as a last resort, to consult his old nurse, a hag who also knew magic. She cast a spell on Finn and the Fianna, to make them invisible, and she herself flew on the leaf of a water-lily which had a hole in its middle like a millstone. She stood up surrounded by an icy cold wind, and started to aim deadly darts at Diarmuid through the hole, which harmed and frightened him more than anything he had known before. Unable to escape, he thought himself on the verge of death. He lay down on his back, protected by his shield Gae Derg, and managed in one last effort to aim his spear through the hole at the hag. She died there and then. Diarmuid cut off her head and brought it to Aengus.

gráinne

After this last combat, Aengus arranged a peace between Finn, King Cormac and Diarmuid and Gráinne. They forgave Diarmuid all he had done during the sixteen long years. And Cormac gave his other daughter in marriage to Finn.

Gráinne and Diarmuid settled far away from Finn and Cormac, in Rath Grainn, territory given by King Cormac. Gráinne bore Diarmuid four sons, and a daughter.

2 The Death of Diarmuid

After some time, Gráinne spoke of her regret that although they lived in such splendour, surrounded by luxury and with a fine entourage, yet they had never received the two outstanding men of Ireland—her father Cormac, the high king of Ireland and Finn mac Cumaill, the chief of the Fianna.

'But they are our enemies!' exclaimed Diarmuid.

'For my part, I would willingly give a big feast, in the hope that you might win their love,' said Gráinne. Diarmuid agreed. Gráinne arranged that her daughter would also invite them to her house, thinking she might find a good husband for herself. After one year of preparations for the two great feasts, messengers were sent to the king of Ireland, to Finn mac Cumaill, to the seven battalions of the Fianna, and to the chiefs of Ireland. They all came and enjoyed those feasts for a year and a day.

On the last night of the feast, Diarmuid was awakened by the voice of a hound. Gráinne threw her arms around him and warned him to beware of the people of the Otherworld: 'Protect yourself, it is the Tuatha Dé Danann doing that to you to spite Aengus. Lie down on your bed again!' Three times the barks of the hound tore him from his slumber. At daybreak, he could not refrain from finding out what was happening. Gráinne advised him to take Manannan's sword, the Móralltach, and his magic shield, Gae Derg. But this time Diarmuid did not listen to her. Instead he took another sword, another shield and his hound Mac an Cuill.

On the summit of Benn Gulban, he met Finn standing before him. Diarmuid did not greet

gráinne

him, but asked him if he had organised the hunt. Finn replied that he had not, but that one of the dogs from the Fianna had come across the track of a wild pig, and had not yet managed to overtake him. He added: 'It is foolish to follow the wild boar of Benn Gulban, since he has already killed thirty warriors of the Fianna. He is now climbing up the mountain towards us. We should turn away.'

Diarmuid said he was not afraid of him and was not going to leave.

'Do you not know you are under a *geis* never to hunt a pig?' said Finn.

Diarmuid did not know it, so Finn told him the story: This boar had once been Diarmuid's foster-brother; it had been prophesied that he would live as long as Diarmuid would and that he would be the cause of Diarmuid's death. 'When Aengus heard that a boar would be the cause of your death, he forbade you to hunt such an animal! It is not prudent of you to wait here for him.'

'I do not know of this *geis*,' said Diarmuid, 'I will depart from this hill, but leave me your hound Bran.' Finn refused to leave Bran with him, saying he had often before let the wild boar escape him.

Alone on the hill, Diarmuid thought that it was to do away with him that Finn had organised this hunt: 'If it is here I must die I have no power now to avoid it.'

When the wild boar came up and rushed towards him, his dog was of no use to him. He regretted not having followed Gráinne's advice: 'Woe to him that takes no heed of the advice of a good wife, for Gráinne begged me early this morning to take my good sword and shield, the Móralltach and the Gae Derg with me.' Diarmuid did not succeed in cutting a single bristle, or making one scratch on the boar. His sword broke in two, his courage dwindled. In the end, he found himself straddling the wild boar which ran down the hill and back up again without being able to dislodge Diarmuid. But eventually Diarmuid fell, and the wild boar sprang at him and ripped out his entrails. As the animal was leaving, Diarmuid in a final effort cast the hilt of his sword at it and killed it on the spot.

When Finn saw Diarmuid near to death, he

gráinne

mocked the loss of his former beauty and attractiveness to women. Diarmuid pleaded with him to save him by giving him water from the palms of his hands: 'When you tasted the salmon of knowledge at the Boyne, you received the gift of restoring youth and health to whoever would drink water from the palms of your hands.'

Finn replied: 'You do not deserve this privilege!' Yet Diarmuid persisted reminding him of the numerous times he had served him well. But nothing could erase from Finn's mind the memory of the night Diarmuid took Gráinne away from him in front of the chiefs of Ireland.

'The fault was not mine, Finn,' Diarmuid went on, 'Gráinne had cast a *geis* on me. I would not have failed to keep my bonds for the gold of the world!' Under pressure from Diarmuid's friends, Finn walked to a nearby well and raised two hands full of water, but twice on his way back to Diarmuid he let the water run through his fingers. The second time it was at the thought of Gráinne. Diarmuid expired before Finn finally came up to him with the water.

The Fianna gave three great loud wails for Diarmuid; then they reached the fort where Gráinne was standing on the rampart. Seeing Finn holding Diarmuid's dog was enough for Gráinne to understand what had happened. The pain she felt was so intense that she fell from the rampart, giving birth to three dead sons. On seeing Gráinne in that state, Oisín sent Finn and the Fianna away. Hearing her three long and piteous cries her people came running to her. 'My heart is heavy that I am not able to fight against Finn. For I would not have allowed him to leave.'

Her people, five hundred of them, on hearing of Diarmuid's death, uttered three long lamentations and these cries were so loud that they were heard as far as the clouds of heaven. Gráinne asked her people to bring Diarmuid's body back. But Aengus would not let them do so. He wanted to take it back to Brú na Bóinne. There was nothing Gráinne could do as she had no power over Aengus.

She sent a message to her children to return. She greeted them with kisses. They sat accord-

gráinne

ing to their rank and age. As they drank sweet ale and strong fermented draughts, the company became exhilarated. Gráinne spoke to them in a clear voice. 'My children, despite a covenant of peace, Finn mac Cumaill slew your father. You must now avenge him. Here is your inheritance from your father: his armour and his various weapons. I will divide them out among you, may they bring you success in battle. I myself will have the goblets, the drinking horns, the beautiful golden cups, the herds of cattle undivided.'

She exhorted them never to be treacherous, or malicious, but to be brave; she instructed them to spend some time in apprenticeship with Bolcan, the smith of the Otherworld. They obeyed their mother and said their farewells.

Finn was filled with fear. He asked the seven battalions of the Fianna for their advice: 'They have gone on that journey with the intention of taking their revenge on me.' Oisín answered: 'The guilt is yours. It is not for us to redress the harm you have done, you were at peace with Diarmuid and then you betrayed him. You have planted the oak, now it is up to you to bend it!'

Saddened, Finn could do nothing against his son Oisín. Realising they had all abandoned him, he decided that the only way he could escape all the dangers that threatened him was to win Gráinne over. He left Almu discreetly without any farewells. Once at Rath Gráinne, he used all his skills and cunning to seduce Gráinne. She attacked him with her sharp tongue and ordered him to get out of her sight. But Finn persisted. Now he desired her body and soul; he wooed her so well with loving words, that at last he won her. Gráinne, following her instinct, gave in to him.

They arrived at Almu together. The Fianna, seeing them together, laughed mockingly. 'We trust, Finn,' said Oisín, 'that from now on you will take good care of Gráinne.'

When their seven years of apprenticeship ended, Gráinne's children returned to Rath Gráinne only to discover their mother's union with Finn. As she had not taken her leave of them they could do nothing. They declared war against Finn.

gráinne

In no time at all, they had reduced a hundred men to three heaps. Finn asked Gráinne's advice. 'I will make peace between you,' she said.

'That would give me great pleasure,' said Finn and he added: 'I would give your children and all their descendants freedom forever, their father's place in the Fianna, all guaranteed to them forever.'

Gráinne went to welcome her children. They accepted Finn's offer and peace was made. They received what Finn had promised. A banquet was prepared and there was much jubilation.

Gráinne and Finn stayed together until death.

On Gráinne

Gráinne is described as a great beauty, although her name means literally 'ugliness'. She is a woman full of spirit and desire. Even though Finn, the head of the Fianna, comes with great pomp to wed Gráinne, a marriage endorsed by her father, she chooses Diarmuid, a well-known warrior and lover of women. Although she had accepted Finn's proposal, she does not feel bound by her word and feels free to change her mind.

Gráinne chooses Diarmuid, but he refuses through fidelity to his leader, Finn, to break his faith and consider her as a possible companion. She puts Diarmuid under a magic bond, a geis, a kind of absolute prohibition whose violation involves a threat of disaster, destruction or dishonour if he does not elope with her as she commands. A geis creates a situation of conflict between two incompatible loyalties, here love and duty. Diarmuid will incur shame whether he goes or stays. Gráinne rejects every one of the excuses made by Diarmuid, refusing

gráinne

to return to Finn as he advises. The geis *shows Gráinne's power and privilege. Diarmuid consults his companions and each in turn submits to the ineluctable injunction of the* geis. *He thus accepts his fate reluctantly, flees with Gráinne, and breaks his bond as a warrior and his allegiance to his chief Finn. In time, Diarmuid will seek Finn's pardon, explaining that he was not responsible for his actions. Gráinne is the one who decides everything.*

With the woman choosing to be taken away by a man, there is also the idea of the 'happy abduction', without violence, by a man enchanted, exalted, who agrees to sacrifice his honour as a warrior for the love of a woman. Gráinne asks a sacrifice for love. And in other ways she governs her desire; she is not obeying a need, she is conscious of the law, but decides to transcend it.

Gráinne's distinctive trait lies in the way she solves a series of conflicts. First, she follows her desire in such a way that she is unfaithful to her own word, to her father, King Cormac, and to Finn, the head of the Fianna, whom she had initially accepted. Gráinne again gives prior-

ity to her desire over her word, thereby displaying a versatile and flexible character, when she conceives an irresistible desire for the magic fruit of the giant's rowan tree. Diarmuid had contracted a truce with the giant under the strict condition of never touching the fruit. But she is determined to eat those berries, come what may. And they are even more delicious when picked from the top of the tree where Diarmuid and Gráinne install themselves after slaying the giant. This is the forbidden tree analogous to other trees in great myths and legends. In this episode we find the same theme as in Grimm's fairy tale, Rapunzel, or in Eve's story as told in the book of Genesis, the irresistible desire for the forbidden fruit. Diarmuid and Gráinne obtain the fruit and install themselves at the top of the magic tree. However, unlike the couple in Rapunzel who are punished by the witch who takes their new-born child away and Adam and Eve who are banished from paradise, in this case the transgression—the breaking of the pact with the giant—inaugurates a brief time of happiness in the tree.

Another of Gráinne's conflicts is that beween

her practical prudence or patience and her impulsiveness. She knows how to survive in the wilderness, away from the luxury of life in the fort, enduring a vagrant life of dangerous wandering. During what seems a very prolonged period, Diarmuid and Gráinne are chaste: Gráinne is patient in the the face of Diarmuid's reluctance—she can wait. But suddenly she throws discretion to the winds. One day, when crossing a river, she taunts her lover, praising the water which laps against her thighs for being bolder than the great but all too abstinent warrior. When the time comes Gráinne follows her erotic desire without compunction.

A third conflict is that between Gráinne's trust and mistrust. She takes heed of the warnings at the beginning of their flight, is greatly alarmed, but Diarmuid feels confident. Once peace is established between Finn and Diarmuid, she suggests a feast inviting Finn and her father Cormac, paying no attention to Diarmuid's objections: 'But we are enemies!' But later when woken by the sound of a hound, she begs Diarmuid not to respond. When he nevertheless prepares to join the hunt, she ad-

vises him to take his best weapons. But Diarmuid does not listen and meets his death.

The fourth example of a conflict is that between Gráinne, the mother, with all the traditional maternal characteristics (she hopes her daughter will find a husband during the big celebration, for instance) and Gráinne, the vengeful woman who commands her children (four boys and one girl) to kill the man responsible for their father's death.

A final example of Gráinne's conflicts and contradictions can be seen in the different versions of the end of her story. One of the endings suggests the triumph of romantic desire: Diarmuid and Gráinne's love remains eternal, as Gráinne remains forever on her own after her lover's death. In another ending, her desire to survive wins: after a period of mourning, Gráinne marries Finn. By this compromise, she becomes the chief's wife and secures for her children the inheritance of their father's place in the Fianna. Gráinne knows how to adapt, how to survive.

Her sovereignty is manifest in that very freedom to change when faced with conflict.

the Daring of Deirdre

One night, the men of Ulster were gathered to drink with King Conor in the house of his story-teller Féidlimid. His wife, who was with child, was serving drinks and food. As time went on, and with the help of the drink, the men started to doze off. While she was preparing to retire, she passed through the centre of the house. The child in her womb let out such a shrill cry that it was heard in the whole fort, awaking the entire assembly.

'Let no one stir, and let the woman explain the meaning of this cry!' said one of the warriors.

Féidlimid asked his wife: 'What is this disturbing cry from your womb, what ill-fate does it foretell? My heart is full of dread and I am already torn with grief.' She turned to Catbad, the druid, and asked him what the shriek meant. Catbad said: 'This shrill cry comes from

Lovers, Queens and Strangers

Growing up away from the men of Ulster, she often walked alone

a young girl whose blond curly hair will fall down her back, whose blue eyes will have a majestic look, whose cheek will have the hue of the foxglove, and her skin the whiteness of a first snowfall. Her teeth will be sheer brightness, and her lips coral red. She will be the most beautiful of all, and the cause of the tragic fate of Ulster heroes. Numerous will be those who fight for her love, the kings who seek her favours. She will flee to the east, seducing a warrior who will leave Ulster: this woman will be beautiful; high queens will be jealous of her; she will be without fault.'

Catbad placed his hand on the belly of Féidlimid's wife's and the child in her womb let out another cry.

'A woman child lies there for sure: her name will be Deirdre, and she will be the source of many sorrows.'

When the girl was born, the young men of Ulster demanded that she be killed.

'No,' said King Conor, 'let her be spared; bring her to me early in the morning. She will be brought up as I command, and later she will be my wife.' The men of Ulster dared not oppose his wish.

Deirdre grew up to be the most beautiful woman in the whole of Ireland. None but her nurse companion, Levorcham, who was also a poet and a satirist, had the right to enter the dwelling where she was being brought up away from the men of Ulster.

One winter day, Deirdre saw a crow land on the snow to drink the fresh blood of a calf that had just been killed. 'Levorcham,' said Deirdre, 'the man I will love will have hair as black as this crow, cheeks as red as this blood, a body as white as this snow.' 'Be happy for you are blessed!' rejoiced Levorcham, 'that man is not far away. He is in the fort of Emain Macha. His name is Naisi, the son of Uisnech.'

'I will not be happy until the day I see him,' cried Deirdre.

Not long afterwards, Naisi, one of Uisnech's three sons, was walking alone on the rampart at Emain Macha. He sang a warrior's lament. On hearing this song each animal gave two-thirds more milk, each man deemed himself happy with his lot. Those sons of Uisnech were brave warriors. They were so skilled at arms

Deirdre

that no man in Ulster emerged victorious from a joust with them. They ran faster than the wind and could easily catch up with their prey.

Deirdre ran towards the singer, but passed him without even a glance. Naisi called out:

'The heifer who runs before me is beautiful!'

'Heifers do well in the absence of bulls,' Deirdre snapped back.

'But the most noble bull in all Ulster is yours, King Conor!' replied Naisi.

'If I were to choose between the two of you, I would take the younger bull.'

'This is not possible for I fear Catbad's prophecy.'

'Do you then reject me?' said Deirdre.

'I do indeed!' he replied.

She suddenly bent over him, seized his two ears, and said:

'Shame on you, and may you be the laughing stock of all if you don't take me with you!'

'Let me go, Deirdre!'

'Certainly not!'

Naisi let out his war cry, and on hearing him every warrior stood to attention. His brothers came to his rescue.

'What are you doing, you'll be the cause of a war between us and the men of Ulster!' they cried out.

Naisi told them what had happened and the shame and derision that awaited him if he did not take Deirdre with him.

'We cannot allow your honour to be at play. We will leave this country together. Wherever we go we will always be welcome.' The brothers departed that very night with Deirdre.

They began by travelling from fort to fort in Ireland. But Conor and the men of Ulster pursued them so relentlessly with their vengeful hatred that they left Ireland. Deirdre, Naisi and his brothers landed in Scotland where they lived in the wilderness. If they missed their prey hunting, they raided the Scots' herds taking a few heads for themselves. The Scots were displeased and rose up against them. The three brothers asked for the king's protection and he took them into his army. For fear of losing their lives if Deirdre were seen by anyone, they built a house for themselves outside the walls of the king's fortress.

One morning the king's chamberlain was taking an early morning walk. He entered Naisi and Deirdre's house and saw the sleeping couple. He ran back and woke the king with these words: 'To this day you have not found a woman worthy of you. But Naisi's wife, the son of Uisnech, is worthy of the emperor of the western world! Have him killed and let the woman share your bed!'

'I will not have him killed,' said the king, 'but go back today to his house and secretly court Deirdre on my behalf.'

So it was done. But every day Deirdre carried the words of the chamberlain back to Naisi. As she was not responding to any advances, the three brothers were sent on increasingly dangerous missions, in the hope that they would meet their death. They survived every peril and the king won no advantage from this scheme.

One day Deirdre learned that the men of Scotland were out to kill the sons of Uisnech. She warned Naisi and added: 'Flee promptly! You will be killed if you do not leave this very night!'

The news of their flight reached the men of

Ulster.

'It is a shame, don't you think, O noble king, that the sons of Uisnech must die in foreign lands because of a dangerous woman. Would it not be preferable that they have your protection in Ireland rather than fall into our enemies' hands?'

'Let them come back,' said Conor, 'send them guarantors of their safety.' The news was carried to them. 'Let Fergus, Dubtach and Cormac son of Conor be our guarantors, and we will come back.' The three men came to meet them. Deirdre, Naisi and his brothers crossed the sea and, under oath not to accept any food before sharing that of the king, they made their way to Emain Macha. But Conor had succeeded in a trick: he had managed to separate Deirdre and the three brothers from their guarantors by obliging Fergus, Dubtach and Cormac to attend a feast. Only Fiachra, Fergus's son, continued with Deirdre and Naisi.

At that time, Eoghan mac Dúrthacht, king of Fernmag, was in Emain to make peace with Conor whose foe he had been for a very long time. In order to obtain this peace, he had to kill the three brothers.

When Deirdre, Naisi and his brothers reached the plain in front of the fortress, Eoghan was facing them backed by the king's mercenaries; the women of Ireland were standing on the rampart. The plain in front of the fort was the scene of a deadly massacre; no one was spared the iron of spear or sword. Naisi met his death when Eoghan's spear went through him, also killing Fiachra who had tried to shield Naisi with his body. Deirdre was brought to Conor, her arms tied behind her back.

Deirdre lived for a year in the palace with Conor. Not once was a smile seen on her face, nor did she raise her eyes; she scarcely ate or slept. If a troop of actors or jesters were invited to perform before her, she would sing her love for Naisi and their life together:

'Far from me the time of laughter, in the proud surroundings of Emain in the east of Ireland. In this beautiful dwelling of merry comfort, there is no peace, no joy, no rest.'

'Who do you hate most, amongst those you see around you?' the king asked Deirdre.

lovers, queens and strangers

'First you, and next Eoghan mac Dúrthacht,' replied Deirdre.

'Then I want you to live with Eoghan for a whole year!' said Conor and he gave her to Eoghan.

The next day, Deirdre was behind Eoghan and Conor in a chariot crossing the plain at the foot of Emain Macha. The king said: 'O Deirdre! Your gaze is like that of a ewe between her two rams—which is what we are for you!'

As they were mocking her, the chariot passed close to a rock. Deirdre threw herself upon it, broke her head and died.

On Deirdre

Deirdre is the Celtic femme fatale and has been called the Helen of the Celtic tradition. It was foretold before her birth that she would be the cause of the ruin of those who loved her. She has a striking youthfulness and vitality. Her story reflects the theme of the young girl brought up in seclusion, far away from human society, with its corruption, rivalry, and envy. In the wilderness, Deirdre is taught by a knowledgeable female companion. This solitude allows her to be formed as an individual entity. Isolated, and in many ways autonomous, Deirdre finds her own law. The will of this young beauty is then confronted with that of the king. Here, Deirdre shows her resistance to any authority which does not emanate from within; she possesses a sovereignty that the power of a king cannot increase.

While still in her mother's womb, Deirdre lets out a shriek, an alarm signal which leaves the entire community stricken with anxiety. The verb derdrestar, *used only once in one of the texts of the legend, seems to mean to cry out. The sound can be associated with the sound of Deirdre. This eerie cry causes Catbad the druid to prophesy that the one who uttered it will be a woman of astonishing beauty and the cause of much violence and suffering among the people of Ulster. Wishing to counteract this prophecy, King Conor resolves to have Deirdre brought up in a hidden place until she is old enough to marry him.*

Deirdre grows up. But when the time comes, she sets out to finds herself a partner without a moment's hesitation. She wishes for the love of an equal, and has no desire for the protective and secure love of a king, however rich. She flees from the court of King Conor with the young Naisi and his two brothers, causing their doom and hers. Thus begin the 'sorrows' which have been linked to her name and which have inspired many writers including William Butler Yeats, John Millington Synge, James Stephens and Donagh MacDonagh.

When Deirdre asks young Naisi to take her away, he recoils: fidelity to the chief of the tribe forbids him to love her. But she binds him by a geis, *threatening him with shame and derision.*

Although his personal honour is at issue, he has to follow her wish. This challenge is stronger than his bonds of obligation and loyalty to his king. One can see in this geis *the irresistible power of Deirdre's call.*

After Naisi's violent death, she spends one year as captive wife of King Conor.

She refuses to be disposed of as a possession or to be exchanged as a commodity. She repels three kings: Conor, King of Ulster, the King of Scotland and finally Eogan, King of Fernmag. Deirdre kills herself rather than submit to Naisi's murderer. For René Agostini, 'It is fate as immanence which is affirmed here: Deirdre chooses her lover, throws him into life and brings him to his death. . . . She does not concede one inch to the king . . . If there is an impression of fate in this play, and first and foremost, obviously, in the myth, this 'fatum' seems to weigh much more at the level of the attachment of Conchubor for Deirdre then at the level of predestination, or of the hold the social order has on the individual (the king chooses his queen), or again of the influence of a psychological disorder (Deirdre despairs *and kills herself).' (*Variations sur un Mythe Celtique, *translated by the author).*

For a young woman who obeys only her own will, to stay for a year with the king is a compromise of her autonomy. But in the end her original self takes over, she prefers death to a situation she can no longer endure. Unlike Iseult in the Arthurian legend, she does not accept her destiny. Unlike Iseult who might say: 'I am what destiny has made of me', Deirdre says, as also would Gráinne, 'I make what I want of myself.' Deirdre refuses to be given to anybody, she cannot tolerate passivity.

the Ruse of emer

One day, Emer, daughter of Forgall the Shrewd, was seated with her companions at the base of his fortress, the Garden of Lugh. She was embroidering, teaching the young women the art of needlework. Suddenly, a magnificent chariot appeared, racing towards them in a fury of metallic sounds, hoof beats, and the creaking of leather straps. It was driven by Cúchulainn, accompanied by his friend Loeg. Cúchulainn saluted the women. Emer raised her eyes and recognised the young hero in his finest garments. 'May God make your path easy!' she said. 'And may you be shielded from any harm!'

'Where did you come from?' she continued. 'Where did you sleep? What did you eat? And what path did you follow?'

Cúchulainn responded in the same enigmatic way. 'I took,' he said, 'the road above the sea, along the Great Secret of the Tuatha Dé

lovers, queens and strangers

'I am the Tara amongst women . . .'

Danann, over the Foam of the Two Steeds of Emain Macha, over the Field of Morrighan, over the Back of the Sow, above the Valley of the Great Ox, between God and his Prophet, by the Washplace of Dea's Horses, between King Ana and his Servant, towards Monnchuile of the Four Corners of the World, over the Big Crime and the Leftovers of the Great Feast, between the Big Vat and the Small Vat, leading to the Gardens of Lugh, to the daughter of Forgall.' He added: 'And you, beautiful one, what have you to say to me?'

'I am the Tara amongst women, the whitest of all, a sentry who has not yet seen anyone. A chaste young maiden is a dragon nobody dare approach. A king's daughter is a flame of hospitality, a road nobody can take. I am surrounded by champions who protect me from anyone who would steal me away without my father's consent.'

Emer challenged Cúchulainn, describing the skills of the champions who protected her, and the amazing power of her father: 'He is stronger than any worker, more knowledgeable than any druid, more subtle than any poet. It is more difficult to win in a duel with Forgall than to win at games, for his exploits are great.'

'Why don't you think me equally able?' asked Cúchulainn.

Emer answered defiantly that if his feats of arms were renowned, she would have heard of them. Cúchulainn promised her that his achievements would be the subject of many tales. He narrated his exploits but failed to impress Emer who saw in them only the deeds of a young boy.

Cúchulainn was, it is true, very young. He had chosen to court Emer when the men of Ulster, angry at the sight of their women languishing after the beardless hero, decided he needed a companion. They were also afraid that he would die without an heir. But after a year of searching, not one of the High King's envoys had succeeded in finding a woman to his liking. Despite the drawback of youth, Cúchulainn was handsome, skilful, audacious, prudent and sweet-talking. Emer, amongst all the young women of Ireland, was the most gifted. She shone in the arts of speech and of the needle. Her gifts made her Cúchulainn's equal.

Cúchulainn was stung by Emer's lack of admiration. 'My foster-father, Conor, raised me well,' he boasted, 'I was brought up amongst champions, druids, poets and noble men of Ulster. I acquired their manners and their gifts.'

Emer asked him to explain who his masters were. He then sang the praises of all those who had educated him, explaining how he had profited from their teaching, and what heights he had reached. After this recital, Cúchulainn asked: 'And you, how were you brought up in the Garden of Lugh?'

Emer spoke of the ancient traditions, of law, virtue, chastity, saying that she was the equal of a queen. Cúchulainn, impressed, said:

'I never before met a young woman with such resolute purpose. Why not join with one another? Why not become one?'

'I still have one question,' said Emer, 'have you got a wife?'

'No,' answered Cúchulainn.

'I cannot get married before my older sister who is here beside me. She is very gifted with her hands.'

'But it is not with her that I am in love!' exclaimed Cúchulainn, 'I have never been with a woman who has known a man before me, and I have heard that she has lain with Cairbre Niafer.'

As they were conversing, Cúchulainn caught a glimpse of Emer's breasts: 'Fair is the valley, nestling between two noble hills,' he declared.

'No one can venture there who hasn't killed a hundred warriors at each ford between Ollbine and Banchuing Arcait.'

'How I like this landscape!'

'No one travels through it,' replied Emer, 'unless he has succeeded in leaping over three ramparts, slaying in one blow three times nine men, without harming the brother in the middle of each group of nine; then bringing each one of them, and my foster-sister, out of Forgall's fortress with our weight in gold.'

'What beautiful scenery!' repeated Cúchulainn.

Emer added: 'No one will be allowed to rest there unless he has managed without sleep from the end of summer to the beginning of spring, from the beginning of spring to the first of May, from the first of May to the start of winter.'

'I will do everything you have commanded.'

'I accept your offer,' said Emer and asked him, in her final question, to describe himself and give his name.

'I am the nephew of the one who becomes another in the forest of Badb, the hero of the plague which falls upon dogs.' With these words Cúchulainn took leave of Emer.

Loeg, on the way home, questioned his friend about the meaning of this mysterious exchange. 'Did you not understand that I was courting Emer?' replied Cúchulainn, 'we had to disguise our words for fear they would be repeated to her father.'

Forgall, hearing of the meeting, did not take long to realise that the handsome young man who had come to visit Emer, and had left for the north, was none other than Cúchulainn. He called him 'the madman of Macha'.

'She has fallen in love with him, but it will come to nothing, I will finish it.'

Posing as an ambassador of the king of the Gauls, Forgall set out for Emain Macha. There he disputed the eulogies of Cúchulainn, pointing out that he had not yet served his apprenticeship with Scathach, the Scottish warrior-queen, without which no warrior's education was complete. This was a stratagem designed to rid him of the young man. Forgall even promised to recompense him on his return, if he came back before a certain lapse of time.

Before leaving for Scotland, Cúchulainn paid a last visit to Emer who, having recognised one of her father's tricks, urged Cúchulainn to be extremely vigilant. They vowed fidelity to one another until they should meet again.

After many tribulations, Cúchulainn, with the help of Scathach's daughter, Uathach, learned the art of war. She advised him how to win over her mother: he must threaten to kill her, a sword against her heart, if she did not grant him three wishes: to teach him her art without fail, to allow him to marry Uathach without a wedding gift, to tell the future (for she was a prophetess).

All this was done, and armed with her teachings, he was victorious in single combat with Aife, the most dangerous warrior-queen in the world. He spared her in exchange for three wishes one of which was that she should spend a night with him and give him a son. After a time, Aife announced she was with child, and that it would be a boy. Cúchulainn named him Connla and asked Aife to send the boy to Ireland when he reached the age of seven.

During Cúchulainn's time of training in Scotland, Lugaid, his foster-brother, a well-known king, wanted to marry. Forgall offered him his daughter, Emer, praising her chastity, her beauty and her skills with her hands. At the wedding feast, as Lugaid sat beside Emer, she suddenly took his face between her two hands and declared that she loved Cúchulainn despite her father's opposition, and that if Lugaid took her he would lose his honour. Lugaid did not impose himself on her and departed.

On Cúchulainn's return from Scotland, as soon as he had recovered from the fatigue of his journey, he went to visit Emer. But for a whole year he was unable to get near Forgall's fortress, it was so well guarded. One day, he came with the scythe chariot he had prepared, made a salmon leap over the three ramparts and landed in the middle of the fort. He dealt a blow to three groups of nine men, each time sparing the one in the middle, Emer's three brothers. Forgall, fleeing Cúchulainn, fell from the height of the rampart to his death. Cúchulainn leapt over the three ramparts with Emer, her foster-sister and their weight in gold. He shed more blood between Ollbine and Banchuing Arcait, as Emer had asked him to do to win her. Thus he fulfilled her demands.

Emer received a warm welcome in Emain Macha. On the night of the wedding, Bricriú, one of the most mischievous men in Ulster, announced that, according to custom, Emer had to spend her first night with King Conor. To calm Cúchulainn's fury (he was, after all, used to being the first everywhere), he was sent to gather the herds of the province. He came back with all the wild animals of Ulster. During that time the wise men found a compromise: Fergus and Catbad would protect Emer from the king during the first night by sleeping with the couple in the same bed. In the morning Emer and Cúchulainn came to know each other. And they stayed together until death.

Years later, Cúchulainns's seven-year-old son Connla came to Ulster. But Cúchulainn had instructed that he should never reveal his name. When challenged to say who he was, the boy refused to answer and Cúchulainn was about to slay him. Emer understood it was Connla and tried to intervene:

'This boy is your only son. Don't kill him! Look at me, hear me! My advice is good. I know his name is Connla, the only child of Aife.' But Cúchulainn did not listen, he killed his son, who revealed his true identity when dying.

One day when Cúchulainn had tried in vain to capture two magic birds for Emer, he fell asleep and dreamed that two women were whipping him, laughing as they did so. Afterwards he fell into into a state of prostration for a whole year. When he recovered, his people advised him to return to the place where he had the dream. There he met Fand, a beautiful fairy who had set her heart on him after her husband, the god Mananann, had been unfaithful to her. He spent a night with her, then they stayed a month together. When he was saying goodbye to her, she said: 'I will meet you wherever you say.' They agreed to meet under a yew-tree near the strand of Ibar Cind Trachta.

Cúchulainn spoke of this tryst to Emer. She prepared knives to kill the young woman, and went to the yew-tree with fifty companions. Fand was already there, and so was Cúchulainn, playing chess with his friend Loeg. Fand noticed the crowd's arrival and said: 'Look! See those beautiful and intelligent women, dressed in tunics held by golden brooches, who are coming with knives in their hands! What a sight! As chariot drivers draw near for the carnage, here comes the daughter of Forgall. How changed she is!' Cúchulainn reassured her: 'Don't be afraid, Fand, you will not be attacked. Sit on my chariot, I will protect you from the women of Ulster. Even though Emer is threatening, she wouldn't dare to do anything in my presence.'

Cúchulainn addressed Emer: 'Wife, I am keeping out of your way, as any hero avoids his friends on the battlefield. No javelin, no knife gleaming in your hand, can harm me. Your anger does not frighten me. How could my power be assailed by a weak woman's strength?'

Emer spoke: 'Tell me Cúchulainn. Why do you dishonour me in front of the women of Ulster, in front of the women and men of Ireland? Am I not under your protection? I know your pride, but what would you gain by leaving me? Why are you doing this to me?'

'What is the harm, Emer, in my meeting this young woman? Is she not beauty, intelligence, dignity itself? Can she not sail on the crest of a wave? Is she not noble, skilful with her hands, charming?'

'The woman you cling to, is she better than me?' exclaimed Emer. 'What shines seems beautiful, what is lacking, desirable, what is new attracts and all that is known seems tedious. Men love what they don't have and what they do possess seems dull. In truth, you have all the wisdom in the world, my friend, if you did but know it. But was there no dignity in our life? If you wish, if I could regain your favour, we could start anew.' Emer's heart was heavy.

Lovers, Queens and Strangers

'Emer,' said Cúchulainn, 'it is indeed you that I want and I shall want you as long as I live.'

'Leave me then!' intervened Fand.

'No, it would be better if I were the one that he abandoned,' said Emer.

But Fand continued: 'No, it is I who must leave.' Her sadness was great. She was ashamed to return home. And the great love she felt for Cúchulainn tormented her. She composed a song in which she spoke of her pain, and of her desire for what cannot be attained.

'Sadness comes to the one whose love is not requited. It is better to depart, unless one is loved as one loves.' She spoke to Emer saying that she should not kill an unhappy woman.

Mananann came to meet Fand when he heard she was engaged in an unequal dispute with the women of Ulster, and that Cúchulainn was leaving her. He was invisible to everyone except Fand. But when she set eyes on him, she was seized with regret. She remembered her past love for him. 'Love is subtle, it disappears easily,' she sang in her lay.

Then she addressed these words to Cúchulainn:

'Farewell. I am leaving with my head high, without rancour. I will not come back. Stay kind, all seems good till departure. I am leaving with my husband, Mananann, he will not turn against me. Do not say I left secretly, look at me, Cúchulainn, if you wish.'

Mananann asked Fand what she wanted: to leave with him or wait for Cúchulainn.

'In truth, you are both worthy of being chosen, one is not better than the other. But it is with you, Mananann, that I am leaving. Cúchulainn has abandoned me. And there is another reason. You do not have a queen equal to you, but Cúchulainn has a queen who is his equal.'

Cúchulainn was astonished by her departure. 'Fand is leaving with Mananann because she did not please you,' explained his friend Loeg. Cúchulainn remained a long time in the south, without food, without drink, sleeping on a mountain.

Emer spoke of Cúchulainn's condition to his foster-father, Conor. He sent his poets and his druids to fetch him and bring him back to Emain. Cúchulainn tried to kill them but they sang magical incantations which bound his hands and feet until he recovered his senses. Cúchulainn asked for a drink. The druids poured him out a draught of forgetfulness. And Mananann shook his cloak between Fand and Cúchulainn so that they would never meet again for all eternity. Cúchulainn had no memory of Fand, or of his past actions. The druids served the same drink to Emer who was no happier than he was. And she forgot her jealousy.

On Emer

Emer is full of wiles. She knows how to veil her exchange with the young man who comes to court her—Cúchulainn, the hero of Ulster, beloved of all the women of Ireland. Emer responds to him in code to baffle her young companions who are embroidering with her. Through those riddles, the two worlds, the terrestrial one and the Otherworld, are evoked at the same time. Without this use of code, Cúchulainn and Emer's intentions would be reported instantly to Forgall, Emer's father, who considers Cúchulainn mad. Forgall does all in his power to prevent their union.

Rather than being flattered by the attention of such a sought-after man, Emer shows her detachment by giving Cúchulainn a great number of tasks to fulfil before she will consider him as a companion. Emer's cunning appears in the near impossibility of what she demands: Cúchulainn has to kill hundreds of warriors, accomplish the feat of the 'salmon leap', kill three groups of nine men without hurting Emer's brothers who are in the midst of these three groups, and he has to go without sleep for months.

Although she praises her father at the begining, Emer does not acknowledge his authority. She does not trust his choice of partner for her and she senses his hostility to her decisions. As soon as Forgall learns that his daughter is welcoming Cúchulainn's advances, he uses tricks to get rid of him. Forgall wishes death upon the man Emer loves, but finds death himself as he leaps into battle against him.

The young woman does more than ignore her father's opposition to her choice, however. She rejects the man he proposes to her in place of Cúchulainn—King Lugaid, Cúchulainn's foster-brother—by the symbolic gesture of the geis. *She takes his face between her two hands warning him that he will dishonour himself if he marries her against her will: she will never love him, she will always love Cúchulainn, and by marrying her he would also oppose Cúchulainn. Lugaid withdraws.*

Emer is Cúchulainn's choice. The men of Ulster, whose women all pined for Cúchulainn, were envious, but having searched the country high and low they could find no one worthy of him. Cúchulainn, having decided to take matters into his own hands, sets eyes on Emer and arrives in grand regalia to woo her.

While Emer waits for Cúchulainn to learn the art of combat in Scotland and fulfil the conditions she imposed on him, he is husband to Uathach, and lover to Aife who bears him a son whom Emer will attempt to protect. Later he falls in love with Fand, a woman from the Otherworld. This last love of Cúchulainn's is the only one to arouse jealousy in Emer.

Knowing of Cúchulainn's love for Fand and of the place of their tryst, Emer comes to meet them with a knife in her hand; but she talks with Fand, and overcomes her jealousy through eloquent words. The dialogue between them shows the character of the sovereign woman. Emer also shows depth of insight in her remarks: 'What shines seems beautiful. What is lacking desirable. What is new attracts and all that is known seems tedious. Men love what they don't have and what they possess seems dull.' Fand returns to the Otherworld without violence or hatred. As in the beginning of her story, Emer shows her intelligence in her recourse to language rather than resentment or envy or hatred.

the isolation of
dervorgilla

Dervorgilla, daughter of the King of Norway, having heard many extraordinary tales about Cúchulainn, set her heart on the young hero. She left her country in the company of a handmaiden. In the guise of two swans, a chain of gold linking them, they set out towards the west and came upon the shore of Lough Cuan.

Cúchulainn and his foster-brother Lugaid, the son of Three Finn-Emna, were walking by the lake. They saw the swans swimming not far from the shore. 'Let's cast a stone at those swans!' said Lugaid. Cúchulainn's aim was so accurate that it went through the wing of one of them and entered her womb. Reassuming human shape, Dervorgilla cried out: 'I was on my way to you! What you have done is very cruel.'

Lovers, Queens and Strangers

'It is so,' replied Cúchulainn, placing his lips to her wounded side. He sucked out the stone which slipped all at once into his mouth with a clot of blood.

'I came from far away to marry you,' she added.

'This is now impossible, beautiful woman,' answered the hero, 'for I cannot join with the one whose side I have touched with my lips.'

'Then give me to the man of your choice!' she said.

Cúchulainn replied: 'I suggest the most noble man in Ireland, my foster-brother Lugaid.'

'Let it be so, as long as I can always see you.' So Dervorgilla joined Lugaid and bore his children.

One day, at the end of winter, a thick snow fell upon the country. The men of Ireland built big pillars with it. The women climbed onto these columns of snow and decided to have a contest saying: 'Let's see which among us can make her water go the deepest. The woman who succeeds in reaching the soil will be the best among all wives.' Not one of them succeeded.

Dervorgilla

Then they called on Dervorgilla who did not like this competition, thinking it foolish. All the same, she climbed to the top of the pillar of snow and her urine went through it right to the ground.

'If our men find this out,' said the women to each other, 'no woman will be loved compared to her. Let's pull her eyes out, cut off her ears and nose and every lock of her hair. Then she will no longer be desirable.'

Having thus mutilated her, they brought her back to her house. The men had gathered on the hill above the fort of Emain Macha. 'I find it strange, Lugaid,' said Cúchulainn, 'that the roof over Dervorgilla's house is still covered with snow.'

'Then she must be about to die,' said Lugaid. They hastened to the house. Dervorgilla hearing them approach, locked the door. 'Open the door, Dervorgilla!' said Cúchulainn.

But instead she started to sing: 'Beautiful was the flower in full bloom when we parted, but now you will not see me again.' She bade them farewell in a fine poem.

It is said that Dervorgilla's soul was no longer

Lovers, Queens and Strangers

in her body when they entered the house. It is also said that Lugaid died on seeing her. In a wild rage, Cúchulainn entered the women's house and tore it down upon them; not one survived. Three times fifty queens, he killed them all.

Cúchulainn had a tomb dug for Dervorgilla and Lugaid, a stone erected, and lamentations sung for them.

On Dervorgilla

Dervorgilla comes from elsewhere. She is a foreigner. But this is not her only distinctive trait. Dervorgilla travels only with her handmaiden, metamorphoses herself into a swan, insists on continuing to see Cúchulainn even after she marries his foster-brother, Lugaid. And most daring of all, she at first refuses to participate in the contest proposed by the women of Ireland. Another token of her difference is that Dervorgilla is forbidden to marry the man she loves: 'I cannot join the one whose side I have touched with my lips,' says Cúchulainn. Could it be that she became his blood-sister when he extracted the stone from her wound and came in contact with her blood? Dervorgilla respects this social law as explained by Cúchulainn but insists on keeping a friendship with him.

Dervorgilla distances herself; she does not participate in the life of the community. She thinks the contest suggested by the women is foolish, her unwillingness to compete displaying a lack of interest in success. But despite her initial reluctance, she finally agrees.

Lovers, Queens and Strangers

Dervorgilla ends up winning: her own urine goes through the pillar of snow and reaches the ground. She thus puts herself in a conspicuous position which prompts the women who organised the contest to plot revenge. No woman should place herself above others.

But there is a contradiction here: on the one hand, the unwritten law says 'you must take part in the contest', on the other, there is a custom that demands that Dervorgilla—maybe because she is an outsider—must refrain from winning, a custom which invalidates the law. Compete to win, but do not win—a double bind.

Was Dervorgilla ignorant of the local custom because she came from elsewhere? The nature of the torture she endured is striking: all her adult facial feminine attributes are torn from her head which is transformed into an oval without definition. Just a mouth, and empty orifices. Winning can have fatal consequences. But Lugaid is faithful to her, and Cúchulainn avenges her.

The enchantment of Edain

1 Edain's first love

One day, Midir came to Brú na Bóinne to see Aengus, his foster-son. He had just arrived when he saw two groups of young men on the point of fighting each other. He tried to separate them, to make peace between them, but in the confusion his eye was put out by a holly branch. Aengus summoned his doctor who put back the eye, and he invited Midir to stay with him for a year. Midir agreed on condition that he be given a cloak worthy of him, a chariot of great value and the most beautiful young woman of Ireland. Midir had heard that Edain Echraide, the daughter of King Ailill, was the most gentle and the most beautiful woman in the country, so Aengus set out for Ulster to ask for her hand in marriage to Midir.

When Aengus made his request, King Ailill

Lovers, Queens and Strangers

pointed out that he would get nothing from the marriage, for if any shame came upon his daughter what redress would he have? Aengus assured him that no harm would come to her and offered to buy her. Ailill agreed and stated his price: 'You must clear twelve plains of marsh and forest so that they become fit for human habitation and for pasture for animals.'

When Aengus had accomplished this task, the king added a new condition: 'You must create twelve rivers, with wells and marshes, so that the riches of the sea may be brought to the people and the land may be drained.' Those tasks completed, Ailill imposed a final condition: 'You will have Edain only if you give me her weight in gold and silver, for up to now everything you have done has been to the benefit of the people and her family.'

'It will be done,' replied Aengus, whereupon Edain's weight in gold and silver was given to Ailill, making him a rich man. Aengus took Edain home with him.

Midir gave them a great welcome and slept with Edain that night. The next day he was given the cloak that was worthy to be worn by him and the chariot he had wanted. Satisfied with his adoptive son, he stayed for a full year in Brú na Bóinne. Midir then decided to return with Edain to Brí Léith where his wife Fuamnach lived. Aengus warned him to take good care of Edain. 'Remember that your wife is waiting for you there. She is renowned for her wisdom and her competence, and more than that, she has my promise and my protection against the Tuatha Dé Danann.' He was speaking of the wise and prudent Fuamnach, who was brought up by the magician Bresal and initiated into the knowledge and magic powers of the Tuatha Dé Danann, the earthly gods of Ireland.

Fuamnach's welcome seemed warm. 'Come, dear Midir, I want to show you your house and the wealth of your land.' And she showed him its abundance. She walked with him around his estate, and showed its riches to Edain too. Then Fuamnach led Edain into her bedroom and said: 'You have come to the seat of a good woman.' When Edain sat on the chair in the centre of the house, Fuamnach struck her with the branch of a scarlet rowan tree. Edain turned into a pool of water. Fuamnach left to join her foster-father, Bresal. Midir, not knowing what had become of Edain, left the house. And from that day on he had no wife.

As the fire on the hearth warmed the air and the ground, the water transformed into a worm which then became a purple fly the size of a human head and striking in its beauty. Softer than the sound of a flute, a harp or a horn was her voice and the murmuring of her wings. At night her eyes shone like precious stones. Her fragrance had the power to turn hunger and thirst away from anyone she approached. The moisture from her wings cured disease in all she came close to. She took care of Midir and kept him company when he visited his lands. She also brought great pleasure and calm to the company at gatherings. Midir, who realized that the fly was Edain, was always happy with her and never felt the need of a wife while with her. Her humming brought him sleep. She protected him from anyone who approached him without love.

After a time Fuamnach paid a visit to Midir; with her came three guarantors, the gods of

Dana. Midir reproached Fuamnach and said that had the powerful gods not been with her, he would not allow her to go away again. She said that as long as she lived she would do all in her power to harm Edain wherever she was or whatever shape she assumed. She knew perfectly well that the purple fly was none other than Edain herself. Was not Midir so delighted with her he looked at no other woman? Unless she was by his side he found no pleasure in anything.

In order to separate Midir and Edain, Fuamnach stirred up a magic wind so that Edain was spirited from Brí Léith and wandered through the air for seven years not finding a summit, a tree or a hill in Ireland to rest upon, but only sea rocks and ocean waves. And then one day she landed on Aengus as he stood on the mound of Brú na Bóinne.

Aengus addressed the purple fly saying: 'Welcome, Edain, careworn wanderer. Fuamnach's cunning has exposed you to great dangers.' Aengus pressed the fly to his heart under his greatcoat. He installed her in his home, in a sunlit, herb-scented room, with windows for coming and going and he gave her purple clothes to wear. He took her everywhere with him, and spent his nights beside her, comforting her. Little by little, colour and happiness returned to Edain. She blossomed in the perfumed atmosphere of her room.

When Fuamnach heard about the love and respect that Aengus was giving to Edain, she said to Midir: 'Ask your foster-son Aengus to come back—I'll make peace between you, and I'll go myself to search for Edain.' On receiving Midir's message, Aengus went to meet him. At the same time Fuamnach took a different route to Brú na Bóinne. As soon as she saw Edain she called up the same wind that had sent her round the four corners of Ireland for seven long years. The great wind chased the enfeebled Edain from the house. She landed on the ridge of a house in Ulster where a large gathering had assembled at table. She fell through an opening in the roof into the golden goblet in front of the wife of Etar, the champion from Inber Cíchmaine, who swallowed her in one draught. This is how she was conceived and was born again as Etar's daughter.

EDAIN

She was named Edain. A thousand and twelve years separated the birth of Edain, the daughter of Ailill, from her second birth as the daughter of Etar.

When Aengus came to visit Midir, Fuamnach had not returned. Midir understood. 'Fuamnach has tricked us. If she finds out where Edain is, she will try to harm her.' 'That's certain,' said Aengus, 'Edain has been with me in Brú na Bóinne for a little while; she is still in the form she had when she was taken from you. Without any doubt, Fuamnach has gone straight to her.'

When Aengus returned home, Edain had disappeared. Aengus immediately went in search of Fuamnach and he found her in Bresal Etarlam's house. He cut off her head and carried it to the outer limits of Brú na Bóinne.

The new Edain was brought up at Inber Cíchmaine in the company of fifty daughters of chieftains. One day, as they were all bathing in the estuary, they saw a man on a brown steed galloping towards them on the plain. He was dressed in a green mantle over a red-embroidered tunic and his hair was the colour of

LOVERS, QUEENS AND STRANGERS

gold. He recited a poem in praise of Edain and then rode off. Nobody knew where he had gone.

Eochaid and his companions saw approaching them a crowd of fifty Edains.

2 Edain's second love

The year after he became king of Ireland, Eochaid wished to celebrate the Feast of Tara, to be attended by all so that tributes and taxes could be assessed. But the men of Ireland declared that they would not come as long as the king had no queen, for it was ordained that no man should come without his wife and no woman should come without her husband.

So Eochaid sent his horsemen, his poets and his messengers through the provinces to the boundaries of Ireland in search of a woman whose beauty, grace and birth would be worthy of a king, and who would not have known another man before him. They travelled from north to south and in Inber Cíchmaine they found the woman they were looking for, Edain, daughter of Etar. The envoys came back to the king with tidings telling of her beauty, youth and nobility.

Eochaid went to meet her. He crossed the green fields of Brí Léith. And on his way, beside a spring, he came upon a young woman. In her hand she held a silver comb encrusted with gold; beside her was a silver bowl studded with bright gems with four golden birds perched on its rim. The young maiden was wearing a red coat over a cloak with silver borders held together by a golden brooch above her breast. Her tunic was green woven silk with red and golden embroidery and shining precious clasps. All who saw her were dazzled. Two braids of golden hair encircled her face and each braid bore a golden pearl.

The young woman let loose her hair to wash it. Her arms were as white as snow, her cheeks the colour of mountain foxgloves. As blue as the hyacinth her eyes, of a delicate red her lips, high, soft and white her shoulders, smooth and white her wrists, and her fingers were long and white, her nails pink. White as snow or seafoam were her thighs, slim, long and smooth as silk. Soft, lissom and white were her legs, slender and straight her ankles, white as foam her feet. Her eyes shone with beauty, and her eyebrows were like the wings of a beetle, the colour of night. She was the most beautiful young woman any human had ever set eyes upon, and for the king as for his companions,

edain

it was as if she had come from fairyland. Later, her splendour would become proverbial and it would be said of her: 'All beauty is in the image of Edain's beauty.'

The king was immediately smitten with love for her. He came closer and asked: 'From what country do you come?'

'The answer is easy', she replied, 'Edain is my name, I am the daughter of Etar of the fairy mounds.'

'May I converse with you?' said the king.

She answered: 'It is to meet you that I came here. For twenty years I have been in this fairy land, my birthplace. Kings and noblemen courted me without success, because you are the one I love. Since I was old enough to speak, I have loved you, because I heard many marvellous stories about you, and though I have never before seen you, I recognise you.'

Then Eochaid replied: 'My welcome for you will be great. I will forsake all other women for you and I will live only with you for as long as you wish'. The young woman answered: 'Let my bride-price be what is fitting and my wish will be satisfied.'

Lovers, Queens and Strangers

'It shall be done as you ask,' said the king and he gave the young woman the price of seven slaves. He then brought her back with him to Tara where she received a marvellous welcome.

Now the king had two brothers, like him sons of Finn: Feidlech and Ailill who was later named Anguba or Ailill of the Single Spot, because the only taint in his life was that he fell in love with his brother's wife.

The feast of Tara was held for fourteen days before Samain and fourteen days after. It was during these festivities that Ailill fell in love with Edain. All day long, he had eyes only for her. Ailill's wife eventually said to him: 'Ailill, why does your gaze wander in the distance for such long hours? Is it a gaze of love?'

Ailill felt shame in his heart and turned his eyes away from Edain's beautiful face. After the men of Ireland had all left Tara, Ailill was still sick with love. He was brought to the fort of Dún Freiman, the favourite dwelling place of the king, his brother. He stayed there for a year, aching with melancholy; but he dared not reveal the source of his pain to any living soul.

edain

One day the king came to see how he was; he laid his hand upon his brother's breast, and Ailill sighed deeply. The king said: 'Your illness is indeed a mystery to us. What is the cause of it?' Ailill answered: 'I do not know.' Then the king called for his doctor, Fachtna, who put his hand on the patient's heart and said: 'You have one or other of the two illnesses a doctor cannot cure: it is either the pain of love which pierces you, or that of jealousy.'

That was the time that King Eochaid had to make his ritual visit throughout Ireland. Before leaving, he said to Edain: 'Be kind to Ailill while he still lives, and should he die, let his funeral lament be uttered, his cattle slain, his grave dug and let a stone be erected upon his tomb with his name inscribed on it.' Eochaid was convinced he would not see his brother alive again.

So every day Edain came to look after Ailill and talked to him for a long time. This eased the young man, and Edain, made thoughtful by Ailill's gaze, asked herself what were the grounds for his pain. His sickness was relieved and he spent hours looking at her. She wondered what ailed him. One day she said: 'Your grief is great. If we only knew what would make you happy, we would help you.' Ailill whispered: 'It is from love of you . . .' 'Had you said so sooner', she exclaimed, 'had we only known, you would have been healed a long time ago!'

'It is not too late, if you are willing.'

'I am willing indeed,' she said.

Edain came every day to look after Ailill, bathing his head, cutting his meat, pouring water over his hands. After twenty-seven days Ailill was healed.

'When shall I have from you what is still lacking to cure me?' he asked Edain.

'You will have it tomorrow, but not in the king's dwelling. I do not want him to be put to shame. Come to me tomorrow on the hill above the court.'

Ailill stayed up all night. But at the hour of the tryst, he fell into a deep sleep, and only woke at the third hour. Meanwhile Edain had gone to the hill to meet him. Before long she saw a man who looked like Ailill approaching. He spoke as Ailill would have liked to speak.

When Ailill woke, his sorrow was great.

edain

When she returned, Edain asked him: 'Why so much sadness?'

'That I gave you a tryst and was not there to meet you. I fell into a deep sleep and I have only just woken. It's clear that I am not yet healed'. But she calmed him: 'Why be distressed? One day follows another. Come tomorrow to the same place.'

But next day, despite the huge fire lit to help him in his vigil, despite the water left at hand for him to bathe his eyes, he again fell asleep at the hour of the secret meeting. Edain again met the man who resembled Ailill, and again found Ailill in despair on her return. She went three times more to the trysting place, and each time, instead of Ailill, she found the same man waiting for her. 'It is not you I agreed to meet,' said Edain. 'As for the man I was to meet here, I do not wish for his love nor do I wish to hurt anyone. I only wish to heal his love sickness for me.' The man said: 'It is I you should have arranged to meet. For when you were Edain, daughter of Ailill, king of Echrad, it was I who was your husband. I left in your place your weight in gold and silver, and created great plains and rivers to pay for your dowry.'

'What is your name?'

'I am Midir of Brí Léith,' he said.

'And what separated me from you?'

'The sorcery of Fuamnach, the spells of Bresal Etarlam,' answered Midir. 'Will you come with me?'

'No,' she said, 'I will not exchange the king of Ireland for a man whom I know nothing of.'

'I am the one who put love for you into Ailill's mind, so that he became thoroughly love-sick. And it was I who stopped him from keeping his tryst, to protect your honour. Come with me to my kingdom if Eochaid lets you go.' 'Willingly,' said Edain.

Edain returned to her house. 'Now I am healed,' said Ailill, 'and yet your honour is safe.' 'It is well,' said Edain.

When Eochaid returned from his travels, he rejoiced that his brother was alive and thanked Edain for what she had done.

3 The Second Wooing of Edain

One lovely summer morning, Eochaid Airem, king of Tara, was looking at the countryside from the terrace of his fort when he saw in the enclosure a strange warrior dressed in a purple tunic. He had golden hair reaching to his shoulders and eyes of brilliant blue. In one hand he held a five-pointed spear, in the other a white-bossed shield studded with gems.

Despite his surprise at seeing him there, the doors of the fort not being opened at that hour, Eochaid greeted the warrior: 'I welcome you, but I do not know you.'

'This is exactly how I hoped to be received when I came here,' said the warrior

'We don't know each other,' replied Eochaid.

'In truth, I know you well.'

'What is your name?'

'My name is not a famous one, I am Midir of Brí Léith.'

'Why have you come here?'

'I want to play chess with you,' he said.

'It's true that I am good at chess,' said Eochaid.

In order not to wake the queen, in whose

house the chess board was kept, Midir suggested they use his board.

Eochaid would not play until a stake was agreed upon. They settled on one suggested by Midir and play began. Midir did not at first put all his skill into the game and lost several times in a row. The first wager was fifty dark grey steeds with dappled blood-red heads and fifty enamelled reins. The second was fifty young boars, fifty swords with golden hilts, fifty red-eared cows with red-eared calves, fifty grey rams, fifty swords with ivory hilts, and fifty speckled cloaks.

Eochaid's foster-father encouraged him to ask for even more, since he was dealing with a man of magic power, so he demanded services of profit to his kingdom. The great tasks he asked Midir to perform were to clear Meath of stones, to plant gorse bushes over Tethba, to build a causeway over Moin Lamraige, and to plant a wood over Breifne. Midir made only one condition: that no one go out of doors before morning. However, one man, a steward instructed by Eochaid, did steal out to watch the work in progress.

edain

Midir carried out all the great tasks, but was angry and complained of the hardship Eochaid had inflicted on him. Eochaid appeased him. When they played again, it was Midir who set the stake: 'The wish that the winner expresses.' That day Eochaid lost the game. Midir then announced what he wanted from him: 'My arms around Edain and a kiss from her'. Eochaid remained silent for a while and then said: 'Come back in a month and your wish will be granted.'

A year before Midir had courted Edain, but could not win her. He had called her *Bé Find* which means 'the woman with blond hair'. This is what he said to her:

> Will you come with me woman of the blond hair?
> to the wondrous land where all is harmony,
> where hair is like the crown of the primrose,
> and the body smooth and white as snow . . .
> O Woman, if you come to my proud people,
> a crown of gold shall be upon your head
> honey, wine, ale, fresh milk, and drink,
> you shall have with me there, O Bé Find.

Lovers, Queens and Strangers

And Edain had answered: 'Only if my husband consents shall I leave with you.'

But when Midir came back a month later, Tara was encircled by an army of the best warriors in Ireland, assembled by Eochaid. The king and queen were in the middle of the house. The courts were locked for they feared the magical powers of the man they were expecting. That night when Edain was serving the wine, something she did in a style of her own, Midir suddenly appeared among them. He had always been handsome, but on that night he was magnificent. The astonished guests fell silent. The king welcomed him.

'I have come to receive what has been promised,' said Midir. 'What I promised you, I gave you.'

'I need more time to think,' said Eochaid.

'Edain herself has promised me that she will leave you,' said Midir. Edain blushed. 'Don't blush, dear Edain,' said Midir, 'There is nothing undignified in that, I have spent a year courting you, sending you jewels, the most beautiful treasures that can be found in Ireland, and I have waited for Eochaid to give his permission.'

'I told you I would not go to you unless Eochaid agreed. You may take me if he says yes.'

'No, I will not give you up!' exclaimed Eochaid. 'Nonetheless, he can put his arms around you here now, in the middle of the house.'

'That's good,' said Midir. He took his weapons in his left hand, and Edain under his right arm, and in front of the dumbfounded assembly they flew through the skylight. Ashamed, the guests made a circle around Eochaid. They saw two swans flying around Tara and then towards the mound of Femuin.

Eochaid made his way there with an army and then on to Brí Leith. Counselled by the wisest men of Ireland, he started to dig up the fairy fort there in search of his wife. It took them a year and three months, because so much of the work done during the day was undone before the following morning.

One day, as the army was attacking the mound at Brí Leith, Midir came towards them.

'What have you got against me? You are doing me so much wrong,' said Midir. 'You assigned me great tasks. You ceded me your wife. Stop harming me.'

'Edain cannot stay with you,' said Eochaid.

'Return home. Your wife will rejoin you tomorrow at the third hour,' said Midir, 'and if this satisfies you do not injure me any more.'

'I agree,' said Eochaid. Midir sealed this covenant and left.

Next day at three o'clock, Eochaid and his companions saw approaching them a crowd of fifty Edains. All were silent. In front stood a woman with grey hair. The women said to Eochaid: 'Choose your wife, or ask one of the women to stay with you. It is time we set off for home.'

Eochaid was so puzzled he asked his companions what he should do. 'We do not know.' they answered. Then he remembered: 'My wife serves drink better than anybody else. I will recognise her by the way she serves.'

Twenty-five women stood on one side of the house and twenty-five on the other, and a jug filled with wine was placed in the centre. One woman after another came to serve the wine.

edain

He still could not recognise Edain. Then came the turn of the last two women. After the first woman had poured out the wine Eochaid said: 'This is Edain, and yet it is not.' He consulted his companions. 'It is she, yet it is not her way of serving.' The other women left. The men of Ireland were satisfied that the king had rescued Edain from the men of the fairy mounds.

But he had made a mistake. One day, Eochaid and his queen were talking to one another in the middle of the court when they saw Midir coming towards them. 'Well, Eochaid, you inflicted great hardship on me,' he complained. 'I did not cede you my wife,' said Eochaid.

'You did not know your wife was pregnant when she left you, she bore you a daughter, and she is the one who is now at your side. Edain is with me, and so you let her go a second time.' On those words Midir departed.

Eochaid had made a covenant with Midir and did not dare attack his mound again. He grieved at having lost Edain and that now his own daughter was carrying his child. He vowed that he and his daughter's daughter would never look at one another. She was cast out

Lovers, Queens and Strangers

and abandoned. A herdsman and his wife found her and brought her up. She grew to be very gifted and in turn became the mother of Conaire, the High King of Tara.

In another version, when Eochaid discovered he had made the wrong choice, he came back to dig up the fairy mound. This time Edain made herself clearly known to him, and he took her back in triumph to Tara.

On Edain

Edain is human and nonhuman. She has two lives, two loves. She is an insect, she arrives hidden amongst fifty indistinguishable replicas of herself.

The first part of the legend tells the story of Edain's life threatened by jealousy. The love between Edain and Midir is described as one of shared trust. This relationship infuriates Fuamnach, Midir's first wife, who is gifted in the art of magic and uses it cunningly against her rival.

A long time after her first birth, Edain the goddess is reborn. This time she is reincarnated as a terrestrial woman and becomes King Eochaid's wife. Edain, whether divine or human, woman or insect, retains the same qualities of attentiveness, compassion and healing. She enchants all those who surround her.

Because she is compassionate, she agrees—during King Eochaid's absence—to meet Ailill, the king's brother, who loves her. But so as not to shame the king, she arranges for the meet-

ing to take place outside the fortress. By this, she shows she is aware that what she is granting is most unusual. Edain has an elusive, mysterious, almost oblique side to her character; but this does not stop her from respecting the law, the code of honour. So she will not follow Midir unless he obtains her husband's consent.

In these legends, some of the characters have a counterpart or rival figure. For Edain it is Fuamnach, Midir's wife. She is understandably jealous where Midir, her husband, is concerned, but what are we to think of her jealousy of Aengus? She is described as a cunning, powerful person versed in the art of magic, her suggestion to call Aengus back shows how she plans and manoeuvres. She calls herself a 'good woman'. She benefits from the support of powerful gods which leaves Edain defenceless against her threats. Transformed into an insect, Edain still retains her singular personality, still pleases the king, so Fuamnach stirs up a magic wind which for many years prevents Edain from finding a resting place. Though less knowledgeable than her rival, Edain has more power of attraction.

edain

In the second part of the story, sovereignty is what King Eochaid needs to consolidate his reign. The men of Ireland only agree to come to Tara, where all are convoked to fix levies and taxes, if the king has a queen. The king chooses Edain who bestows sovereignty.

'Eochaidh had become king, but his kingship could be validated only by his union with the goddess of sovereignty, in this case Edaín. This union of king and goddess was at one time ritually enacted at the Feast of Tara' and if he had not sought out Edain to be his queen 'he would have been the supreme paradox of a king without sovereignty', writes Proinsias Mac Cana in Celtic Mythology.

But even if Edain is the symbol of sovereignty, we may ask: what exactly is it she wants? At the beginning of the legend, on meeting Midir, the Otherworld king, she appears to be in love. She cares for him and accompanies him during his walks. Later, she also seems to love his foster-son, Aengus, the one who sought her out. What relationship has she with him? Is he just a mediator, a third party, merely preparing the way for the two lovers to meet?

Fuamnach lets us know that there might not be a completely peaceful relationship between Midir and Aengus.

Clémence Ramnoux has summed up Edain's story in Le Grande Roi d'Irlande*: 'The first story is spun out around a cast of four in the world of fairies: two fairy gods, an older king and a younger one; two fairy women, one pursuing the other on earth with her jealousy. The first drama ends in a legend of nativity. One finds in it the theme of the wind carrying germs of a fertile nature, the woman impregnated by an insect swallowed with some water. Thus begins Etain's human story.' She makes this comment about the way Edain was conceived: 'The theme is found in many stories of birth: amongst them the birth of Cuchullin, the hero. . . . It is a primitive image of conception, found in other folklore and in childish images of birth. Modern psychoanalysis has identified the image of the worm, or the serpent, as a symbol of the male organ, and noted amongst certain women the fear of water as a vehicle of sexual penetration.' (Translated by the author.)*

In her life on earth, Edain seems to love

Eochaid. And even though she admits having no love for Ailill, the king's brother, she nevertheless agrees to meet him secretly—to heal him thoroughly of his love sickness. Clémence Ramnoux continues her résumé: 'In the second part of the legend, on earth, Etain is again the object of a double amorous rivalry: first between royal brothers; then between the fairy man substituted for the royal lover, and the High King. The rivalry between the brothers, in Tara, is matched by the rivalry between the fairy-gods, Midir and Mac Ind Óg (Aengus's other name), around the same Etain, the fairy-woman. This rivalry is a transversal one, so to speak, between the man and the fairy-god. However, the fairy-god only gains access to the woman (in this case a fairy re-born as a woman), under the double condition of taking the shape of a man (here the lover), and of obtaining her from the husband, in this case through a wager at chess.'

Finally, in the third part, which of the two kings who fight to win her does she prefer, Midir or Eochaid? She agrees to follow Midir if he obtains Eochaid's consent. Two endings *to the story point towards two answers. In one, she would choose Midir because under the guise of fifty Edains, she remains inaccessible to King Eochaid, and does nothing to reveal herself to him. It seems that Edain intends her future to be determined by Eochaid's capacity to seek her out. Or is she making herself indistinguishable amongst the multiple figures of herself so as to remain in the Otherworld? Is Edain passive? What does she want? Her choice seems to be to remain with the one who wins, the one whose determination to have her is strongest. Having obtained Eochaid's consent (to put an arm around Edain's waist and steal a kiss from her) Midir will win Edain back. But she does not collaborate. On the contrary, she blushes with shame when Midir intimates to Eochaid that she has participated. She agrees to change lovers on condition it is above board, 'legal', following convention. In the other version, she finally reveals herself, and Edain and Eochaid ride back to Tara in triumph.*

What does she wish? To live with Midir or to remain as a queen with Eochaid? Will she say 'yes' to the one who makes the greatest effort to obtain her, to the one whose desire is obviously the strongest? Is her desire subject to the desire she inspires? Can we read her answer as a 'yes'? The double ending does not offer a definite answer.

We could replace the question by the following observation: Edain loves the choice of the moment; she loves Midir and she also loves Aengus; she loves Eochaid and Midir. Edain loves several people, she loves variety, metamorphosis. She has two sides, even multiple ones. She has two lives, two metamorphoses (into an insect and into a swan), two lovers in each of her lives: Midir and Aengus in the first, Eochaid and Midir (in the shape of Ailill, the king's brother) in the second.

Edain's first metamorphos is into a pool of water, which under the maturing action of the fire, becomes a worm, then a vividly coloured insect whose size varies: first that of a human head, then small enough to be swallowed by Etar's wife. Each corporeal shape is submitted to the constant possibility of metamorphosis. Is it significant that the word cuil, *insect in Gaelic*, is so close to col, *the Gaelic word for transgression, incest, which becomes* cuil *in the genitive form. Where would the transgression lie? Once ingested, re-born, Edain is rid of the 'insect' side of herself.*

There are two metamorphoses, the first into an insect, the second very brief, into a swan, when she flies out with Midir through the aperture in the roof. The last transformation into fifty Edains is not exactly a metamorphosis, but a multiplication which makes it more difficult for Eochaid to repossess her.

There are two loves in the two parts of the legend. In the first, Midir loves Edain. Edain loves Midir. But as he has not taken his first wife's outrage into account, Edain is transformed. Aengus welcomes Edain and cherishes her. But she disappears again and leads a solitary roaming life before being swallowed and reborn. In her second life, the human Edain will be loved by the High King Eochaid. But obliquely, through Ailill, who falls ill of a love sickness for Edain, Midir courts her again. When the fairy-lover of the first romance reveals himself to the human Edain, she does not remember him, having no recollection of her

EDAIN

former life. Nevertheless she agrees to follow Midir if her earthly husband agrees. This time, she does not encounter a jealous competitor nor end up alone and miserable; she has a choice: life in the Otherworld with her first lover, Midir, king of the Otherworld, or in the royal fort of Tara with King Eochaid.

At the end of the first part of the legend, Edain is sad and diminished. She can't find a place to rest, is torn from one place to another, tossed around by winds for seven years. In the third part, Edain vanishes into the Otherworld. She reappears to human eyes. Has she gained more freedom? Has she greater sovereignty? If the love of the first story ends in bewilderment is the second love happier? Could it be that the love story, started in the first life and abruptly halted, is completed during the second episode? If Edain is separated from Midir in the first part of their love story, the outcome of the second part remains ambiguous. The version presented above is the one in which Edain and Midir remain together.

Bibliography

The main sources for the stories in this book are marked *.

Agostini, René *Deirdre, Variation sur un Mythe celtique, J. Synge, J. Stephens, D. MacDonagh* Editions Artus, 56200 La Gacilly, 1992

* Bergin, Osborn and R. I. Best *Tochmarc Étaíne* Royal Irish Academy, Dublin, 1938

Bourke, Angela *The Burning of Bridget Cleary: a true story* Pimlico, London, 1999

Chalier, Catherine *Les Matriarches, Sarah, Rebecca, Rachel et Léa* Les Editions du Cerf, Paris, 1985

Condren, Mary *The Serpent and the Goddess, Women, Religion, and Power in Celtic Ireland* Harper & Row, San Francisco, 1989

* Cross, Tom Peete and Clark Slover (eds.) *Ancient Irish Tales* George Harrap & Co., London, 1937

Dumézil, George *Mythe et Epopée* Gallimard, Paris, 1971

* *Ériu* n°5, 1911

Heaney, Marie, *Over Nine Waves, A Book of Irish Legends* Faber, London, 1994

* Kinsella, Thomas *The Táin* Oxford University Press, London, 1970

Bibliography

Mac Cana, Proinsias *Celtic Mythology* Hamlyn, London, 1970

'Women in Irish Mythology' *Crane Bag Book of Irish Studies, 1977–1981* Blackwater Press, Dublin, 1982

MacCurtain, Margaret 'The Religious Image of Women', *Crane Bag Book of Irish Studies, 1977–1981* Blackwater Press, Dublin, 1982

Mhac an tSaoi, Máire 'Margadh Na Saoire' in *An Cion go dtí Seo* Sairséal Ó Marcaigh, Dublin 1988

Markale, Jean *Petit Dictionnaire de Mythologie Celtique* Editions Entente, Paris, 1986

Ní Bhrolcháin, Muireann 'Women in Early Irish Myths and Sagas', *Crane Bag Book of Irish Studies, 1977–1981* Blackwater Press, Dublin, 1982

Ní Dhomhnaill, Nuala *Selected Poems* Raven Arts Press, Dublin, 1988

Ó Cathasaigh, Tomás 'Between God and Man: The Hero of Irish Tradition' *Crane Bag Book of Irish Studies, 1977–1981* Blackwater Press, Dublin, 1982

Ó hÓgáin, Daithí *Myth, Legend & Romance, An Encyclopedia of the Irish Folk Tradition* Prentice Hall Press, New York, 1991

* O'Rahilly, Cecile *Táin Bó Cuailnge* from the Book of Leinster, Dublin Institute for Advanced Studies, Dublin 1967

Ramnoux, Clémence *Le grand roi d'Irlande*, Editions de L'Aphélie, Céret, 1989

Rees, Alwyn and Brinley *Celtic Heritage, Ancient Traditions in Ireland and Wales* Thames and Hudson, London, 1961

Sjoestedt, Marie-Louise *Gods and Heroes of the Celts* Turtle Island Foundation, Berkeley, California, 1982

Sölle, Dorothée, Joe H. Kirchberger and Herbert Haag *Great Women of the Bible in Art and Literature* William B. Eerdmans Publishing Company, Grand Rapids, Michigan, 1994

Von Franz, Marie-Louise *Interpretations of Fairytales* Spring Publications, Dallas, 1970

The Feminine in Fairy Tales Spring Publications, New York, 1972

Warner, Marina, *From the Beast to the Blonde, on fairytales and their tellers* Chatto & Windus, London, 1994

Managing Monsters: Six Myths of Our Time (The Reith Lectures 1994) Vintage, London, 199e4

8 witrsw